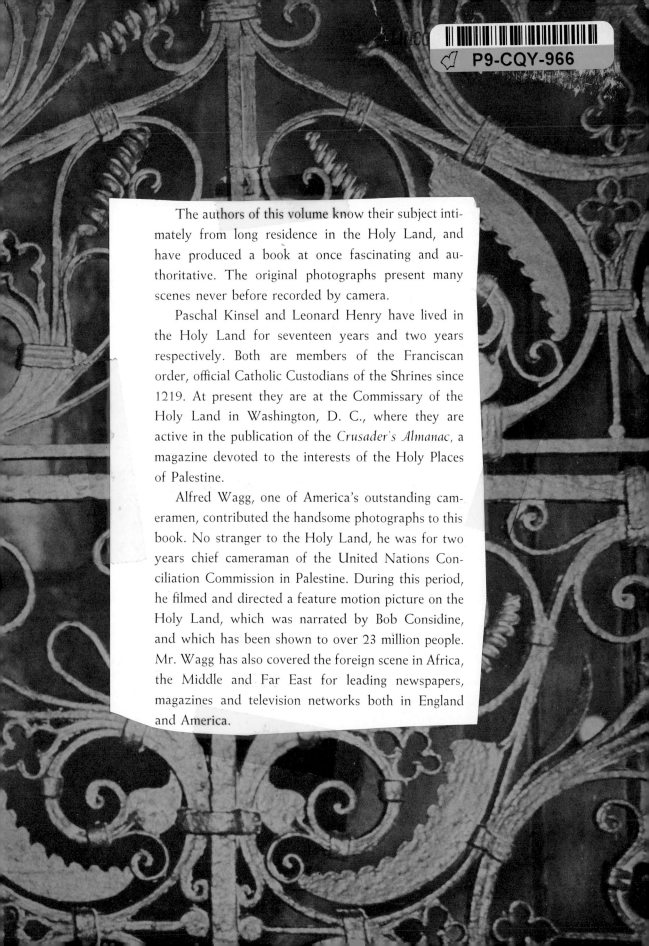

The authors of this volume know their subject intimately from long residence in the Holy Land, and have produced a book at once fascinating and authoritative. The original photographs present many scenes never before recorded by camera.

Paschal Kinsel and Leonard Henry have lived in the Holy Land for seventeen years and two years respectively. Both are members of the Franciscan order, official Catholic Custodians of the Shrines since 1219. At present they are at the Commissary of the Holy Land in Washington, D. C., where they are active in the publication of the *Crusader's Almanac*, a magazine devoted to the interests of the Holy Places of Palestine.

Alfred Wagg, one of America's outstanding cameramen, contributed the handsome photographs to this book. No stranger to the Holy Land, he was for two years chief cameraman of the United Nations Conciliation Commission in Palestine. During this period, he filmed and directed a feature motion picture on the Holy Land, which was narrated by Bob Considine, and which has been shown to over 23 million people. Mr. Wagg has also covered the foreign scene in Africa, the Middle and Far East for leading newspapers, magazines and television networks both in England and America.

*Palm Sunday procession in Jerusalem with the Garden of Gethsemane,
Basilica of the Agony and Mount of Olives in the background*

The Catholic Shrines of the Holy Land

End Papers: *A gate near the Shrine of the Annunciation in Nazareth*

The Catholic Shrines of the Holy Land

By The Very Rev. Paschal Kinsel and The Rev. Leonard Henry

With photographs by Alfred Wagg

FARRAR, STRAUS and YOUNG Inc. New York

Second Printing, July 1951

Imprimi Potest
Fr. Hyacinth Faccio, O.F.M.,
Custos of the Holy Land
Jerusalem

Nihil Obstat
Fr. Anthony S. Rosso, O.F.M., Ph.D.,
Censor Deputatus

Imprimatur
✠ *Patrick A. O'Boyle, D.D.,*
Archbishop of Washington, D.C.

Book designed by Nelson Gruppo

THE AUTHORS gratefully acknowledge the permission of Sheed and Ward, Inc. (the publishers), and of His Eminence, Bernard Griffin, Cardinal Archbishop of Westminster, for the use of quotations from Msgr. Ronald A. Knox's translation of the Scripture as they appear in his books *The Old Testament* and *The New Testament*. The authors are similarly indebted to Longmans, Green & Co., New York, and Eyre and Spottiswoode, London, for permission to use material from Henry Daniel-Rops's *Sacred History*.

FOREWORD

AVING SPENT seventeen years in the Holy Land, it is almost like writing about my own country in preparing a foreword for this latest book on Palestine. In many respects my knowledge of that little country, about the size of the state of Vermont, is more comprehensive than I could possibly have of our own vast United States.

Much has been written on the homeland of the Bible by those who have never seen the Holy Land nor understand its many complicated unsolved problems. Others have repeated the same prejudicial views that crop up periodically. As presented in this book the Holy Land emerges a living reality in word and picture.

The manuscript was prepared by Reverend Leonard Henry, a Franciscan of the Commissariat of the Holy Land, and a member of that international group of brown-clad Sons of St. Francis, who have been the faithful guardians of the world's most sacred heritage for the past seven hundred years. Living as a missionary and instructor in the Holy Land, Father Henry often visited the biblical sites, villages and other places of interest. He taught the youth of that land, Jew, Christian and Moslem, mingling freely with the various classes and religions. Hence the story he presents remains free of bias and partisanship.

The illustrations are from the photographic collection of Mr. Alfred Wagg, himself an author of four books. Mr. Wagg spent some eighteen months, 1949–50, in the Holy Land where he visited in every section of that country. His keen appreciation of ceremony and ritual has resulted in his securing scenes rarely or never taken before. The combined efforts of these two, author and artist, have produced a book which should make the Bible better known and treasured.

The Holy Land is ever essentially the same—sacred because of God's frequent visitations and because it is the Son of God's birthplace. Often has it been bathed with the blood of thousands, slain in the wake of feuds and wars. What the final solution of the present status will be no one can tell. Within the pages of this book there is a graphic portrayal, not of conflict, not of conquest, but of what the Holy Land is and why the Franciscan custodians refer to it as the "Pearl of the Missions." There they have remained, unshaken in their task, armed only with the weapons of love for Christ and charity for all mankind. Plague, famine, pestilence, earthquakes and wars cannot swerve them from their path of duty and loyalty for the land of Christ.

Catholic Shrines of the Holy Land tells that epic story—tells in a simple way the joy and peace there is in serving the country of Christ without fear or political ambition. With reverent forthrightness and frank impartiality the author has presented a new and enlightening picture of a very old and vital subject. May its light guide you to a better understanding of a very complex question.

VERY REV. PASCHAL KINSEL, O.F.M.,
Commissary of the Holy Land,
Washington, D.C.

CONTENTS

INTRODUCTION

The Little Strip of Land forming the eastern barrier of the Mediterranean, known as the Holy Land, has an impressive history. The reason for this lies in the amalgam of nations and tribes who have occupied that land for the passing centuries. Three thousand years before Christ, the Semitic Chanaanites left their colony on the Persian Gulf and settled in the fertile farm lands of Syria. And another branch of this race, the Phoenicians, came to the coastal region along the Great Sea while the Amorrhites settled near the Lebanon.

Ten centuries later Abraham led his people along established caravan routes from Chaldea into what is now Hebron, some twenty-eight miles from Jerusalem. This was the land promised by God to the Patriarch and his descendants forever. Chanaan then came to be known as Israel among the Jews, as later it would be Palestine for the Romans.

The country covers a little more than ten thousand square miles in a wedge that is sixty miles wide in the south and twenty miles across in the north. Syria, Lebanon, the Hashemite Kingdom of Jordan, and Egypt form the land frontiers with the Mediterranean sweeping the entire coast line on the west where the ports of Haifa, Tel Aviv, Jaffa and Acre localize maritime commerce.

The climate varies from the subtropical in Jericho to temperate weather in Galilee and the arid deserts around Gaza and Beersheba. There are only seven cities with populations exceeding twenty thousand; of these Jerusalem, Tel Aviv and Haifa are in the lead. The country is now divided between the governments of Israel and Jordan.

Palestine was called the Holy Land by God when He spoke with Moses (Exod. iii) and it was considered to be richly blessed since it was the country of the Patriarchs Adam, Noe, Abraham, Isaac and Jacob. It was the home of the Kings Saul, David and Solomon and the center for the Prophets Isaias, Jeremias, Ezechiel and Daniel. So many friends of God lived in the land: Job, Tobias, Judith and Ruth as well as the Twelve Apostles, Mary and Elizabeth. Jerusalem was the location of the great Temple, Calvary and the Dome of the Rock Mosque, places where God has been worshiped through many centuries.

Palestine has witnessed the devotion of saint and zealot; the bravery of warrior and wanderer; its treasures have fallen to king and tyrant; it has seen the tides wash up the refuse of East and West as well as the worth while; it has quickened the imagination of missionary and knight-errant; it has been coveted and conquered in times past and its visitors have ranged from God Himself to the avowedly godless. The land has been blessed and cursed, praised and parodied; it has inspired courage and enthusiasm side by side with indifference and cynicism; it is a land of contrasts where strong,

Map of the Holy Land as it is today showing the location of many of the towns mentioned in the text. The white area indicates a large portion of modern Israel

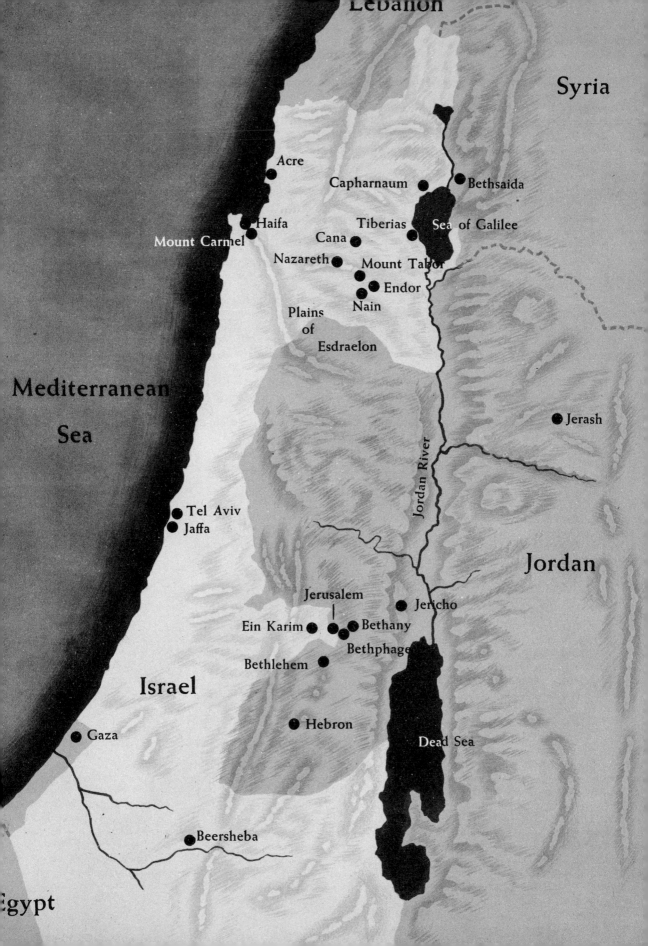

opposing races intermingle but do not assimilate.

Three outstanding religious groups, a monotheistic triangle formed by Jew, Christian and Moslem, claim Palestine to be their spiritual homeland. This trio, distinct in fundamental concepts of the Deity, diverse in creedal expression, divided as to racial attitudes, is unanimous in asserting Palestine to be their unique spiritual heritage. Such convictions are supported by the sacred chronicles of each sect as well as the history symbolized in shrines and memorials and the love they have for this "land all milk and honey, the best of lands." Ezech. xx, 15.

The Jordan River

As an interlude before introducing Palestine there is the city of Jerash, in Transjordan. This city with its unrivaled and well-explored ruins affords a concrete picture of Roman life in the Middle East just before and following the birth of Christ. Known then as Gerasa, the city was settled by Semitic farmers and shepherds who soon saw it was advantageous to become citizens of Rome. When Palestine surrendered to Pompey, 63 B.C., the place was known as Antioch, and was a rival to Philadelphia, now Amman. It was also a member of that confederation of cities called the Decapolis and it is believed that Marc Antony gave the city to Cleopatra as a gift.

Jerash was occupied for a time by the Syrian Nabataeans who made their influence dominate the commerce and culture. When they departed the Romans came and by the year 150 A.D. the civic development was completed and the golden age of the city flowered. During the Roman period some of the city's finest architecture came into being. The Fountains of the Propylaea, the Temples of Artemis and Zeus, the North Theatre and the West Baths are regarded as an excellent expression of the gifted and energetic Roman rulers.

Christianity came to Jerash about 150 A.D. and for the next century there are records of martyrs. The apogee of the Christian epoch came toward the end of the fifth and the beginning of the sixth centuries. Ten churches and a great cathedral were in Jerash, all built on basilican lines. The cathedral fronted on a famous fountain that was reported to send forth wine instead of water on the feast of the Epiphany, Twelfth Night. The chronicles state that a two-fold commemoration was achieved in this unusual happening: the first miracle performed by the Saviour in Cana and the visit of the Magi to Bethlehem were kept thereby before the people.

The city was destroyed extensively by the Persians who occupied the land from 614–628 A.D. Then came the Moslem conquest in 635, and after this the transfer of the capital from Damascus to Baghdad. The precarious living in such a remote place and a series of earthquakes caused Jerash to be abandoned with only the ruins to bear witness to the elegance of bygone days.

The Crusaders came to the city but left neither memorial nor building. On the other hand, there is no record that the Moslems ever converted any Christian churches into mosques. William of Tyre visited Jerash in 1122 and stated that the city had been desolate for a long time, an observation which was mentioned by Yaqut in the following century. Nothing more is written concerning Jerash until the mid-nineteenth century, when it was "rediscovered." In the thousand years it lay deserted the only ones who came near the city were those who sought material with which to build their dwellings in the nearby villages.

Crossing the plain that leads up to Jerash the first glimpse one

The ruins of Jerash. In the background is a modern Circassian town

A window box, dating back to the early Christian era

18

*Jerash temple pillars. Extensive ruins
dating from the time of Christ may still be seen*

*Dome of ancient bath in Jerash,
standing for some 2000 years*

sees is the stately, yet lonely-looking, Triumphal Arch, which bears traces of Roman and Hellenistic civilizations. The Temples of Artemis and Zeus, the amphitheatre, the well-preserved baths, the forum, pavements and mosaics attest a well-planned and functional city. The Christians, however, did not build with the same precision and all the churches have fallen into ruins. Examination of the buildings has turned up many Greek and Latin inscriptions, numerous pieces

Imposing exterior of the ancient baths in Jerash

Roman ruins at Jerash, with temple in background

An amphitheater in Jerash

of sculpture, wall decorations and an unusually fine glass cup which may have been a chalice.

Jerash, away from the highways usually taken by visitors, remains little known. While it is not a shrine it does reflect the grandeur of Rome and it is, even in its desertion, one of the finest of old cities. So often, because of the circumstances attendant on the birth of Christ and the poverty that is associated with Bethlehem, there is a tendency to regard all Palestine in the same perspective. There was a splendor in living among the Romans and where they colonized they left the enduring monuments of a culture that ranks among the greatest. Jerash, built and embellished by the same Romans, became a spot of beauty and elegance in the harsh plain. Thus the Romans prepared the way for the Christian era not only with buildings but in management, legal systems and the Pax Romana. Upon Greek culture the Romans engrafted their own to produce that which has been enjoyed and adapted ever since. This is to be seen in Jerash and Jerusalem.

Jerash prepares a pilgrim for Jerusalem. In the former city there are abundant evidences of ancient Roman opulence and a this-worldliness, while in the latter there are evidences not only of the mundane, but of a presence linking today with yesterday. Both cities attained eminent degrees of civilization; both suffered from enemies and the elements; each one witnessed its conquerors finally defeated and their peoples dispersed. Jerash, in ruins, may well represent the temporal and transient while Jerusalem, the Holy City, rises (as did the Saviour) gloriously from defeats—the city that cannot be hidden, that cannot be forgotten, "an inheritance for the race that serves him, a home for all true lovers of his name" (Ps. lxviii, 36).

G OD, OR YAHWEH, begins the history of the Chosen People when Abraham and his nephew Lot were directed to come into the land of Chanaan, west of the Jordan, extending from "Dan to Beersheba." Isaac his son, and Jacob the grandson, extended the boundaries of the land. The former introduced methods of agriculture which brought about a radical change of living and the latter was given definite assurance that the race would continue and increase. Wars followed the rather peaceful occupancy of the land and the people were brought into slavery by the Egyptians. Moses, their deliverer, was singled out to lead his people back into the Promised Land. As he was dying he selected Josue to be his successor and the command was given "to cross yonder stream of Jordan, taking the Israelites with thee into the land I am giving them for their own . . . I will be with thee as with Moses, never leave thee unbefriended." Jos. i, 2, 6. During the forty years the Jews wandered in the desert a national unity was achieved and their religious aspirations now crystallized into monotheism, which made them unique among the other tribes.

Josue's advance was not without some opposition in the cities of Jericho, Hai and Lachis, but these strongholds in Chanaan ultimately fell and then conquest was rapid. The tent now gave way to fixed abodes and the nomads settled down in peaceful possession of the land. Government was confided to a few leaders while the religious life and its interpretations came under the supervision of the priests.

The new growth with all its blessings was not without that one bane which would inhibit constantly Israel's relation with God, the infiltration of paganism. This would cause serious and repeated lapses from the God who had favored them. Struggling against the common enemy Israel's fervor was exceptional. But with good fortune the people, who had recently been participants of heavenly largess, would forget and repudiate the Deity only to be left abandoned and crushed with new defeats. Then, and only then, did they find Yahweh. By prayer and humiliations the nation was strengthened and leaders brought forth to make them great among the tribes of the earth.

After Josue, who divided the land among the Twelve Tribes, there came another period of deterioration and leadership passed to the Judges. Many a saintly figure graced this epoch; Debbora the prophetess ruler of her tribe; Gideon, who defeated the pillaging Midianites; Samson the Strong and Ephraim the Levite all labored to hold the nation within the confines of religious fidelity.

Samuel came as the last of the Judges, leading his people through the many wars with the Philistines when the Ark of the Covenant was captured. Saul, chosen to be the leader by Samuel, lived up to all Hebrew expectations. In the three decades of his reign victories

26

followed and he organized the army into an effective defense unit.

David, armor-bearer for Saul, came next to the throne. After attacking the Jebusite city, Jerusalem, he was acknowledged the master. His rise was phenomenal. He rebuilt Jerusalem, had the Ark returned, planned to build a temple and the city became "an impregnable fortress" in which was centered both civic administration and the seat of religious worship. The kingdom extended from the Red Sea to the Euphrates and was to last until 240 A.D., when the Persians would become masters. David brought Israel into its most glorious phase.

Rocky Mount Moriah in the northern part of Jerusalem was purchased from one Areuna, a Jebusite, who had a threshing floor on its summit. This was where David planned to build the Temple, but for all his desires that honor would go to his successor. A succinct biography of David appears in the appraisal of Daniel-Rops, "A soldier full of valor, a poet whose work has come down to us, decisive in politics and chivalrous in war, determined in his undertakings, feeling deeply in his personal relationships, he has every quality that makes a man lovable, even those which make him like ourselves and for which we love him the more—those weaknesses through which a man is prone to fall, and which, in a noble mind, are themselves the occasion of sorrow, repentance and forgiveness." (*Sacred History.*)

Solomon followed David and his reign was known for its splendor, peace and prosperity. He was endowed with exceptional juridical and intellectual gifts and he is mentioned as being the author of the Book of Proverbs, Book of Wisdom and Ecclesiastes. Judgment and political acumen were evident in the first years of his administration but there was a general weakening in the latter years induced by accentuated lasciviousness.

Solomon, aware of the wish of David, began to build the Temple on a scale hitherto unknown. Tens of thousands of men were em-

Rabbis teaching young Jewish students. The covering of the head, worn inside the home, school and synagogue, is prescribed

ployed to quarry, carry and set the stones and "the whole building, beam and pillar and wall and doorway was faced with none but the purest gold . . . a brazen altar, carved doors, lamp-stands and the place for the Ark." The heart of the nation thrilled with this tangible expression of devotion, the Holy of Holies.

In the midst of all this luxury troubles were brewing, and with the death of Solomon the kingdom separated into Judah in the south and Israel in the north. Discord, division and jealousies so weakened the land that it was easily overcome by the armies from Damascus, Assyria and Egypt. Three centuries later the Holy City was sacked, burned beyond recognition and its people led back into Egypt as slaves. As they traveled and mingled with other nations there developed within the Jews the impetus toward corporate courage even while bitterness filled their homesick hearts.

The messages revealed by successive prophets began to bear fruit and Israel was again converted to the God who had shown so much mercy and who had delivered them from their harsh masters. Aware of her new destiny and led by the Maccabean princes, the nation defeated the Macedonian invaders. Sixty-three years before the birth of Christ independence was lost to the Romans. Pompey took Jerusalem but placed the government in the hands of native princes of whom Herod the Great was the best known.

Despite all the misfortunes that came to the Jews they clung to that one basic truth, the Oneness of God. His word remained fixed amid all the superstitions they had encountered and his religion was proposed for this race alone. God's covenant would last forever, Jerusalem would be their city. Rebuilt again and again, there would be a day when suffering was done and the Temple "most famous in all the world" would be, in their midst, a symbol of divine favor.

As long as there are Jews upon the earth these beliefs will be maintained. God, who gave them the Land and derived so much honor from worship there, must be thanked forever. The Jews of

30

Students in an Orthodox Talmud school in Jerusalem.
Over 500 students from the ages ef four to seventy-two attend this school.
Pupils never "graduate," but stay as long as they wish.
Side curls follow the Talmud law against using a knife on one's beard

31

Palestine are united with their co-religionists throughout the world, especially when they gather at the Wailing Wall in the Holy City.

This bit of Wall is all that remains of the outer western wall of the temple built by Herod. It is reached by a winding way through little dark streets, down slippery steps and under covered passages. On turning a corner there it looms, a great barricade of white limestone. The Wall is about one hundred feet high but only half of this is above ground. The lower part of it is made up of courses of stone from the Herodian period. Above these are later Roman courses and nearer the top they are of a much later date. In the crevices between the blocks grows some sort of shrub, but to call this the hyssop mentioned in the Scriptures is erroneous. Along the length of the Wall a number of iron nails are inserted. They have been placed there by pious pilgrims who wished to leave a remembrance of their visit, an incentive, no doubt, arising from the book of I Esdras ix, 8, "Now has our prayer been made before the Lord . . . to leave us a remnant, and give us a pin in his holy place."

When the temple built by Herod was destroyed all the sacred appointments were scattered, the Jews were driven out and later the entrance was forbidden to them. On the other hand, because of a persistent tradition concerning the treasures from the temple which were said to have been buried in the locality, not a single Orthodox Jew would set foot within the precincts. A compromise was reached so that those pious Jews who wished to pray as close to the temple site as possible (yet remain without ceremonial defilement) began to gather at that part of the sacred edifice still standing, called The Wall of Wailing. This is the symbol of Israel's longing, a rallying point. Once, when visits to the Wailing Wall were permitted (before that section of the city passed over into Jordan territory), the Jews could be seen huddled at the base of the rampart, praying, weeping and sometimes bemoaning the loss of their temple and repenting of their personal transgressions. The Wall, menacing, im-

The Mosque of the Dome of the Rock, built over the place where a tradition says Abraham offered his son Isaac, and where the sacrifices of the Old Law took place

*A Greek Orthodox Archbishop and Assistant
officiating at the ceremonies of Holy Week in Jerusalem*

passive and symbolic, made those below seem forlorn and tragic, but their faith kept alive their belief in the divine presence which still hovered about this lone relic of Israel in the Holy City. On any day there used to be Jews at the Wall, but the great attendance would be on the Sabbath eve and just preceding the high holy days.

Besides the Wailing Wall, Jewish sympathies are directed to the Tomb of David, said to be on Mount Sion;* that of Rachel near Bethlehem; the sepulchres of Abraham and Leah in the Hebron Mosque. The biblical towns of Tiberias, Capharnaum and Haifa; the provinces of Samaria, Judea and Galilee; as well as the ruins of the ancient synagogues—all have an especial place in the heart of every child of Abraham. The Jews, however, do not remain idly gazing upon the past. Israel has come to the land with well-planned scientific methods and now the desert blossoms like the rose. Trades have been revived, new industries have appeared. The Jewish university offers advanced courses in medicine, arts, sciences and archeology. A lively export trade has been established and the fame of Palestinian citrus products has spread through Europe and the British Isles. What the future holds for the new state of Israel no one can predict with surety, but one thing is obvious and indicative of the achievement—these Jews love the land and are dedicated to it by their lives and labors.

Long ago the plaintive song of the Jewish captives in Babylon sounded the keynote: "Jerusalem, If I forget thee, perish the skill of my right hand! Let my tongue stick fast to the roof of my mouth if I cease to remember thee . . . the fountain-head of my content." Ps. cxxxvi, 5–6. This could be the motif of the present day builders of Israel as their work goes on in the twentieth century.

PALESTINE is holy to the Jews but it is equally holy for the Christian world. It is the land where Jesus Christ was born, where He localized his social and philanthropic activities and where He died.

* Greek transliteration Hebrew *Zion* (*Tsion*).

35

Modern Israeli shoemaker in Galilee

Bedouin

37

Shrine, memorial and monument dot the country, each reflective of some phase of that Man who changed the destiny of men and nations.

Mingling with the conspicuous minarets and ancient synagogues in the land are the domes and spires crowned with the Cross of Christ. These are churches, residences and institutions striving to carry out his mission and his mercy. Nazareth, Bethlehem, Tabor, Gethsemane, Ein Karim, Bethany, Tiberias—what a host of recollections stirs when this litany rolls from the tongue of a Christian!

Christianity in Palestine had three epochs—that which followed on the Resurrection of Jesus, that which came to be identified with Crusader rule and that which is known and lived today. Christ when he preached the Sermon on the Mount (Mt. vi) concluded with a simile concerning the wise man who built on the firm foundation of a rock. The Master was building his church on the foundation of Peter, chosen to be head of the Twelve Apostles. The first of the Fishermen was given extraordinary powers for this task after he acknowledged Christ to be "the Son of the living God." The Church founded in Palestine was not to be localized and Peter centered his activities in Rome. In the city of the Caesars the Cross of Christ would be triumphant as it was in the city of the Herods.

The young Church in Jerusalem was made up of converts from Judaism and at first was not distinct from the synagogue; in fact, there were definite attempts made to reconcile the words of Christ with the Jewish ritual. Discontentment and antipathy resulted and the rift grew into persecutions, during one of which the Deacon St. Stephen was martyred.

With the growing distrust for the religion of Christ the beginnings of the missionary movement came into being. These new Christians set out from Palestine and traveled into other lands, thereby fulfilling the Saviour's directive that his religion was for all peoples and for all times. In the Palestinian Church there came a predominance of

The Wailing Wall, sacred to Jews, is part of the outer wall of Solomon's Temple

Syrians until the fourth century. By then the influence of Constantinople had extended and many Greeks came to Palestine. In the following century there grew up doctrines at variance with those taught in the established Church and, despite the effort to bring about unity of belief, the cleavage grew, aided and encouraged by leaders interested in nationalism. The breach widened until in 1054 the Eastern Church finally separated from the jurisdiction of the Church established in Rome. Among the major controversies was that of Papal supremacy. Those who refused to acknowledge the Pope as Head of the Church came to be known as the Greek Orthodox; those who subscribed to the teachings of Rome came to be called Greek Catholics or Uniates.

The same distinctions may be found in Palestine even in our days, when the word Orthodox with its descriptive adjective mentioning nationality means one who does not accept Papal authority in spiritual matters. Thus there are Armenian, Coptic and Abyssinian Orthodox and the same sects may be Catholic or Uniate if in communion with Rome.

The Roman Catholics of Palestine who use Latin as the language for religious worship are called Latin Catholics, while two other groups of Catholics are the Maronites so named from their founder, St. Marron, and the Melkites who are descended from early Catholics of Syria and Greece.

When St. Jerome came to Palestine in the fourth century he founded monasteries in and around Jerusalem. Three centuries afterward the monks of St. Benedict arrived and were established in abbeys throughout the country. The real impetus to religion came earlier when St. Helena, mother of Constantine the Great, made a pilgrimage to the Holy Land and saw the sorry condition of the places connected with the life of Christ. She began excavations, built large churches and small chapels in order that these sites would not be forgotten. In fact, most of the Holy Land shrines that remain

A fisherman of today mends a net by the Sea of Galilee

are the result, direct or otherwise, of the labors of this holy queen who had nothing much to start with save the local traditions. St. Helena's visit did much to awaken the West to the importance of the land of the Saviour.

From a religious point of view Jerusalem became the center of a great revival from the fourth to the seventh centuries. Many churches were erected, monks and sisterhoods came from the West to open monasteries and convents which were the only places of education, and the advancement of sacred art moved along with the growing population. In 614 the city was attacked by the Persians and in 638 it was taken by the followers of Mohammed.

The new Arab rulers were tolerant toward the Christians, and in 807 the caliph of Baghdad, Haroun el Raschid, sent the keys of the Holy Sepulchre to Charlemagne as a token of consideration. Unfortunately this amity was disrupted in 1010 when another Caliph, Hakim, destroyed all the Christian monuments. The shock of such desecration as well as the spread of Islam and the tales of treachery and bloodshed, aroused Europe from apathy to fear. The popes were gravely concerned but it was Urban II, in 1095, who launched that offensive which was called the Crusades. The object was to deliver the Holy Land from oppression and to free the Tomb of Christ from the Moslems. Never before had there been such a response as knights, soldiers, peasants and adventurers set out to liberate Jerusalem, traveling the entire way on foot except for ferrying across the Bosphorus and the Adriatic Straits.

The Crusaders adopted as their distinguishing badge a red cross worn upon the breast and this was later incorporated into the garments of the Knights Templar. From the standards flew the Five-fold Cross, a large cross of red with four smaller crosses above and below the transverse arm. This became the coat of arms of the Latin Kingdom of Jerusalem and is part of the major seal of the Franciscan Order whose cherished field of activity is the Holy Land.

A Crusader's Cross carved in the wall of a temple at Jerash

Four years after the Crusaders left Europe they entered Jerusalem, took possession of the Holy Sepulchre and set up a Christian government, with Baldwin of Edessa crowned King of Jerusalem in 1100. The city was again lost in 1187 and all its sanctuaries except the Holy Sepulchre were demolished in 1219. A decade passed when the truce between the Emperor of Germany, Frederick II, and the Sultan of Egypt, Melek el Kamel, was respected and Christians returned to Jerusalem, but in 1244 they were massacred and all future sultans continued the policy of hostility.

From the years 1096 to 1244 eight crusades were inaugurated, each one attempting to achieve a lasting victory in Jerusalem. Most important of all was the first with nearly a half a million people marching over Europe, united under the leadership of Godfrey de Bouillon. The succeeding calls of Christendom never seemed to excite the same spirit nor arouse the interest that had been fanned by the zeal of the first preachers.

A few Christians continued to reside in the Holy Land but after the fall of Jerusalem they risked mistreatment and persecution and were often sold as slaves. Under the Mamelukes, in 1382, new restrictions were enforced that Jews and Christians had to wear identifying headdresses, yellow for Jews, blue for the Christians. However, those who remained as a sort of underground Church were encouraged by the promise of the Founder that He would be with his Church all days. The intrepid men and women who kept the faith eked out an uncertain living near shrine and sanctuary. They were taxed heavily and sometimes a few concessions were bestowed on them. These proved valuable when England acquired mandatory powers over the country in 1917 and so often considered these grants as the basis for settlements of protocol problems.

"The blood of martyrs is the seed of Christians." Never was this truer than in the chronicle of Palestine, where the heroic sacrifices of soldiers and leaders are preserved. They traveled long distances

A street scene in the Old City of Jerusalem

to struggle for a country called, and with reason, the Holy Land. The Crusaders, a medley of nations, brought to Christendom an awareness of its unity and purpose, while their subjective bravery produced holiness in many lives.

That same spirit is found today wherever there are Christians. They turn with longing toward the country of Christ and though a visit may not be possible, they can still relive the days when Europe marched under the banner of the Cross to the land of the Cross. Jerusalem can yet become our happy home when there courses through humanity's heart a mutual esteem "which is the root of all spiritual *rapprochement*" and when we become ennobled in purpose by the Prince of Peace, who died in this land that we might live abundantly.

MOHAMMED, an Arab merchant (570-632 A.D.), whose influence was to be so far-reaching, preached a new religion in the Arabian desert near the Red Sea. This religion, Islam or "The Acceptation," made many converts and the zeal of newly won masses spread to the north and west. The adherents of the Prophet came to be called "The Believers." Fundamentally the chief tenet of this cult is the Unity of God. Nearly all "that had seemed difficult to the untrained masses; the Trinity, the Incarnation . . . the Sacraments . . . and the priesthood" were eliminated. Within a century after the death of Mohammed, 732 A.D., his religion had swept through India, China, Spain and southern France. In the eleventh century it absorbed what was left of dismembered Christianity in Palestine and from 1244 until the surrender of Jerusalem, 1917, Moslems were the rulers.

When Islam conquered a land many of the inhabitants were converted to doctrines which seemed credible for a convinced monotheist. Beyond the Unity of God much religious speculation was permitted and the small number of easily discharged observances

A Moslem shepherd boy tending his flock

appealed to many. It was not long until Palestine became the Asian stronghold of Mohammedanism and Jerusalem became "El Kuds," the Sanctuary, the Believers' second holiest city.

This religion promised the land to all Believers, and the Christian shrines and churches, when not demolished or ransacked, were made over into mosques. There were a few exceptions, notably the basilica in Bethlehem. All non-resident Moslems were urged to make a pilgrimage to Jerusalem after they had visited Mecca. The spiritual treasures to be gained for this journey would be heaven and the merits of one thousand martyrs. If one could not perform the pilgrimage he could provide oil for the lamps in El Kuds, and as long as they burned the donor would be remembered in the prayers of angels. One prayer said in the mosque in Jerusalem was worth forty said elsewhere. To kneel eight times while praying meant companionship with Abraham, ten times, association with David.

The mosque referred to is the best known Moslem shrine in the Holy City. The Dome of the Rock is seen in all the panoramas of Jerusalem as the dark, sapphire half-circle dome surmounting the Mosque built in the area where the Jewish Temple once stood. Faithful Moslems gather there for prayer, and the five prostrations toward Mecca are made at almost any hour of the day. Until the mid-nineteenth century none but a Believer could enter the area. Today the restrictions apply only on the feasts of Islam.

This mosque, bearing traces of Byzantine architecture, is octagonal and "stands up like a peacock, lustrous with mosaics that are like plumes of blue and green." It covers a large rock which from the time of Abraham formed the base of the altar of burnt offerings. A little channel can still be seen on the side which carried off the blood of animals. This rock has been mentioned variously as the altar David erected after he bought the threshing floor from Areuna, the Jebusite; as the center of Herod's temple built just before Christ; as the place from which Jesus drove the money-changers and where

49

A minaret of Haram-esch-Scherif, "The August Sanctuary,"
one of Islam's holiest places and site of the Dome of the Rock

he preached so graphically the prediction of Jerusalem's destruction when there would not be left a stone upon a stone. The Romans turned the place into a temple to Jupiter, and Julian the Apostate attempted to rebuild the temple on this site. After that it became a mosque; in time of the Crusaders a Christian church, the Templum Domini; and after they quit the land, it reverted to a mosque and has remained such ever since.

The present building is almost one thousand years old and proclaims "across the valley the victory and the glory of Mohammed." Entering the mosque, the way leads through several vestibules and finally into the rotunda, which looks like a forest of colored marbles, columns crowned with gilded capitals, glass tiles, intricate and highly decorative arabesques and heavy Persian carpets. The grille that

Ancient arches in the Temple area near the Dome of the Rock

50

A fountain near the Dome of the Rock where the faithful Moslems wash before praying

Camel herdsman   *A carpenter uses modern equipment to build boats*

leads into this area beneath the dome is wrought iron made by the French in the twelfth century and within is a circular wooden paling enclosing the bare rock.

The interior of the Dome gleams with rich paintings, and the red and gold tones seem almost like magic brushwork. Light comes from fifty-six pointed windows made of tiny bits of colored glass, red, blue, yellow and green, set into plaster frames with beveled edges of like tints. The artistic arrangement resembles flowers of jewels toned down by a perforated tile screening which admits just enough light to be translucent. Between the pillars of the shrine hang tiny lamps of clear glass arranged in clusters of five or seven. The doors date from the Crusaders' occupation and are of the usual heavy iron hammered into pleasing patterns. The outer part of the

52

Dome is covered with lead and a tall gilded crescent surmounts the highest part.

The Dome of the Rock rises over a mass of natural stone yellowish in color and about five feet high. It is the actual summit of Mount Moriah, a spur of rock standing as it did when Solomon first enclosed it. For a time it served as a Christian altar but very little trace of that epoch remains.

There are many legends about the Rock. One says that beneath it is the Pit of Souls, a cavity where departed spirits come twice a week to do honor to the one God, Allah. The relics exhibited in the mosque include a golden casket containing two hairs from the Prophet's beard, his sword and standard, and one of his footprints frozen in a stone slab. A collection of Korans wrapped in costly damasks and some ancient tiles prove interesting.

The entire enclosure is called the Haram-esch-Scherif and was known as "The Most Distant Sanctuary" (i.e., from Mecca), a name that is now given to just one mosque in the esplanade. There are many interesting shrines in the temple area: the spot where Mohammed's steed was tied the night they both flew into Jerusalem from Mecca; the projecting column from which will be strung a single horse hair over to the brow of Mount Olivet on Judgment Day. (Only those who safely navigate such a perilous crossing will be welcomed into Paradise by the Prophet.) The Gate across the outdoor pulpit is the site where the actions of just and unjust will be weighed; the many little niches for prayer, all appropriately dedicated—one where Mohammed conversed with angels, another where Fatima, his daughter, made her devotions; a place where the Virgin Mary spoke with the Lord and the spot where she cradled Jesus. Inside the door of the el-Aksa Mosque, under the pavement, is the last resting place of some of the murderers of Thomas à Becket, Archbishop of Canterbury. The epitaph, now totally effaced, translated read thus: "Here lie the wretches who martyred the blessed

Thomas, Archbishop of Canterbury." This story of the pilgrimage of the knights, and their death at Jerusalem, is, by many writers, believed to be a legend. There is another story following Jewish traditions—that this spot is the center of the world and the dust for Adam's body came from here.

The temple area is not, however, the only holy place in Jerusalem for Moslems. Standing alongside each mosque are the slender towers called minarets into which the muezzins—those who call the hour for prayer—climb five times each day. Some of the more frequented

Story teller in Bedouin tent

mosques are those in what was Pilate's courtyard and that adjoining the Holy Sepulchre and named for the Caliph Omar who conquered Jerusalem. He was visiting in the Holy Sepulchre one day when the call sounded for the Moslem's hour of prayer. Omar left the spot at once and offered his prayers a short distance away for, said the pious Conqueror, if he had prayed in the Tomb of Christ the followers of Islam would have turned the Sepulchre into a mosque and expelled the Christians. The others are on the Mount of Olives in the place of the Ascension and that of Nebi Daoud (St. David) on Mount Sion in the place of the Cenacle.

The summons to prayer that rouses the Moslems sees them unfold the prayer rugs, face Mecca and do honor to the One God "in that holy city which is the new Jerusalem. . . . Here is God's tabernacle pitched among men; he will dwell with them, they will be his own people, and he will be among them, their own God. He will wipe away every tear from their eyes, and there . . . will be no more sorrow; those old things have passed away." Apoc. xxi, 2, 4. With Jews and Christians the Moslem voices join in testimonies in "Jerusalem, holy city of our fathers." Dan. iii, 26.

Jerusalem, holy city for the three great religious groups, holds a definite place in the heart of the world. Year after year tourists come to Palestine and are baffled at what they see, angered by some of the oft-repeated tales, even scornful of some things. Yet, allowing time in which to understand the history that revolves about Jew, Christian and Moslem, there will come a tolerance of judgment and an appreciation for these sects so dissimilar but whose spiritual tenets begin in the accord, there is but one God and to him does "this world and all that is in it belong." I Cor. x, 26.

CHRISTIANITY came to earth in Nazareth, a little village in that hilly section of Palestine called Galilee. The Virgin Mary and Joseph, to whom she was engaged, lived there. The town, unfortunately, was not a very distinguished one. It does not appear in the Old Testament records and its mention in the New Testament is far from complimentary. Nazareth seems to have been a byword suggestive of the questionable character of the villagers. "Can anything that is good come from Nazareth?" was the question Nathaniel put to Philip (Jo. i, 46). Yet it was this hamlet selected by Jesus Christ as the place in which He became man.

In the centuries before Christ's coming there had been prophecies concerning the Messiah. Daniel furnishes an approximate date: ". . . a period of seven weeks must go by, and another period of sixty-two weeks, between the order to rebuild Jerusalem and the coming of the Christ to be your leader." Dan. ix, 25. The traditional use of the word "weeks" is taken to mean periods of forty-nine years, thus within four hundred and ninety years the Saviour would be born. Isaias had even detailed a "sign the Lord will give you. Maid shall be brought to bed of a son, that shall be called Emmanuel." Isai. vii, 14. Hence, when the Angel Gabriel was sent by God into Nazareth "where a virgin dwelt" there was nothing obscure or confusing in his greeting, withal it was perplexing to the young Mary. "Thou (Mary) shalt conceive . . . and shalt bear a son, and shalt call him Jesus. He shall be great, and men will know him for the Son of the most High; the Lord God will give him the throne of his father David, and he shall reign over the house of Jacob eternally; his kingdom shall never have an end." Lk. i, 31–34. When the miraculous possibility was vouchsafed Mary her accord brought heaven to earth. The Redemption long awaited now began. "Behold the handmaid of the Lord; let it be done unto me according to thy word." Lk. i, 38.

With that expressed fiat, Nazareth became great among other places in Palestine and would be associated forever with the Virgin's commission and the boyhood of the Galilean who came "to do the will of Him who sent me." Jo. iv, 34.

Nazareth as a name has several meanings. There are some who maintain it means a "flower-bearing shoot," others, delving deeper into semantics, maintain it is a "guardian." However, Nazareth, the cradle of Christianity, was both the custodian of heaven's richest treasure and the stalk on which would blossom, like Aaron's rod, the finest flower of earth.

At the time of Christ, Nazareth was just a small Jewish village and remained so until the fourth century. With the arrival of St. Helena in Palestine, the religion of Jesus became more important. Following the local traditions, this dauntless queen proceeded to unearth the localities that had been associated with Christ's life. In each spot dignified buildings were raised up so that the Master's name, his miracles and his activities would not be forgotten.

It is not known whether St. Helena came to Nazareth but it is certain that her son, Constantine, caused the first basilica to be built, 326–336, on the spot where the angelic message was delivered to Mary and where she was called "The Mother of God." A few granite pillars are all that remain of this memorial. When the Crusaders arrived in Palestine in 1100, Tancred came to Galilee, rebuilt the church destroyed by Saracens, and had it dedicated for the newly appointed bishop. Almost simultaneously, a party of Greeks put up a church close to the Virgin's Fountain and called it St. Gabriel's. When the Crusaders left the land in 1291, the fortunes of the Christian communities became increasingly parlous.

There was nothing compassionate in the Moslem occupation— it was either conversion or decapitation. The land was cleared of churches and where such buildings could not be easily converted into mosques they were leveled. Force does not always repel force and just fifty years after the departure of the Franks there arrived in Nazareth a small group of men whose strength was from the Lord Jesus. This army of the Saviour, armed only with the activating love of Christ, was the first contingent of Franciscans. Sons of Saint Francis of Assisi, these men began their glorious adventure in Palestine, 1217, which continues, amid difficulties as always, even in these days.

Nazareth was a sacrosanct spot for those Franciscans. They had learned the intensity of Christ's love for man from their Founder who had come to Palestine as a pilgrim—and it was their joy to begin living amid the ruins of the Annunciation Church, where the Saviour had begun his earthly days. Three hundred years later the confreres of the first Friars would build above the Grotto a church and monastery one of the outstanding Catholic shrines in all Pales-

Main altar at St. Joseph's Franciscan Church, the Church of the Nutrition

tine. The church as it appears now was constructed in 1730 and during Napoleon's battles in the coastal region was used as a hospital for the wounded.

The present basilica of the Annunciation is only about one-third of the original. The entrance is over a large paved court whose stones are worn and shiny from the millions who have crossed them to pray. The long rectangular nave of the church ends with a choir and central altar, under which is the crypt. At the time of Christ and before, the residents of Palestine often used hillside caves as homes, shelters and hiding places. This fact is sometimes overlooked by visitors or those who are critical of the shrines. St. Mark's Gospel, the fifth chapter, makes this very obvious, and the studies prepared by archeologists who have made excavations affirm this.

Many of the hillside dwellings in Nazareth had two rooms. The inner was hewn from the rocky mountain, the outer, terrace-like, was built of branches and clay. The Virgin's home was one of this kind.

The Grotto itself has been cut from rock but is almost hidden by the addition of decorative marble panels. It has an impressive altar whose canvas reredos commemorates the Annunciation while underneath the table the white stone disc bears the engraved message:

"HERE THE WORD WAS MADE FLESH."

This is the sacred spot where the salutation, since repeated thousands of times daily, was spoken, "Hail, thou who art full of grace; the Lord is with thee; blessed art thou among women." Lk. i, 28.

Two reddish granite pillars support the rocky roof in this crypt and have been called "The Column of the Virgin" and "The Column of the Angel." The former has been broken off near the base— all that remains is the upper section suspended from the masonry. This vandalism was done by Moors who hoped to find treasure.

Back of the altar is a semi-circular chapel dedicated to St. Joseph, and under a trap door there is shown the mosaic floor of the ancient basilica.

In such a treasury of faith as Nazareth there are many smaller memorials of the Holy Family's residence. In one end of the walled garden is St. Joseph's Workshop where the growing Boy learned his trade. From earliest days there has been a succession of churches on this site. Recent excavations have brought to light parts of the seventh- and twelfth-century buildings. The present church is Romanesque, with three aisles and a dozen finely colored windows. The open timbered roof covers the crypt which was first called "The Church of the Nutrition." Over the altar the painted panels depict the Holy Family, and the bits of mosaics, cisterns and Crusaders' walls are interesting remains.

When St. Joseph's church is filled with devout Arab parishioners it is a colorful pageant. The billowing costumes, accented with rich embroideries, the voices raised in unfamiliar hymns are convincing enough that there *is* good in Nazareth, good in the people and in their present-day religious teachers—a good that must be attributed to Christ whose birth sent forth from this country comfort and consolation for all.

The Shrine of the Annunciation and the Workshop of St. Joseph are linked together by the spacious monastery of the Franciscans. When this was being constructed there were some who thought it was too large but that feature has been most advantageous. During the past war Nazareth was a refugee center and many homeless men and women of Poland found shelter, food and protection within these stout walls. It has served that purpose again for many poor Arabs who have come into the little town and, being needy and without the help of friends, they turned, as did their forebears, to the sons of St. Francis to find brotherhood, kindness, clothing and even living quarters in part of the monastery property.

Looking down into the Place of the Annunciation

VERBUM CARO
HIC FACTVM
EST

*Marker beneath the altar shows the traditional spot
where the Archangel Gabriel appeared to the Virgin Mary
in the house where she lived before she was married*

*Place of the Annunciation with painting showing the scene.
The present church was built on this site
in 1730, where a Constantinian basilica stood*

"Man cannot live by bread alone." Lk. iv, 4. He must have water too, and in Nazareth the main supply issues from the Virgin's Fountain, known as Mary's Well. This little spot, a few minutes from the Workshop of St. Joseph, has been mentioned over and over in the records of travelers. There are some who claim that this was flowing in the time of Christ. At any rate it is the gathering place for the women and girls who exchange their versions of village events and their observations about the staring tourists. Their wit is both copious and pungent. The array of containers is arresting. One can see jugs of many shapes, pitchers and ewers whose duplicates are kept in museums; and last but by no means to be despised, are the ubiquitous tin cans that once contained oil or kerosene from far away America. Nothing—absolutely nothing—is discarded in the Holy Land, nor is anything considered too old, unless it has passed beyond all conceivable use. It is more than just imagination that adapts some things to a purpose never intended or expected by the designers.

Jesus and his family, being practicing Jews, attended the specified services in their own synagogue. In Nazareth such a place is shown. In the sixth century mention was made of a place where Christ taught on the Sabbath and an alphabet from which He learned to read was also displayed. These have long since disappeared. An account in the Gospel of St. Luke (iv, 14–30) merits some attention. On one occasion when Christ had entered his home synagogue and attempted to explain a passage from the prophet Isaias concerning His Messianic mission, the congregation became annoyed. Their resentment had been smoldering for a long time. Reports of the many miracles He had performed in Capharnaum aroused these local zealots, who thought their hamlet was being ignored. Thus, when the Master clearly identified his work as divine, limitless yet often restricted due to a lack of faith in his hearers, this was considered a personal affront. "No prophet finds acceptance in his own country" was the sad commentary of the Nazarene concerning his kinsfolk.

Monsignor Anthony Vergani watches the nuns feeding children

The Church of the Visitation. Mosaic shows Mary
with guardian angels traveling from Nazareth to Eim Karim,
where she visited her cousin, Elizabeth, mother of St. John the Baptist

Altar of the Holy Family in the crypt of the Church of St. Joseph in Nazareth

IC ERAT SUBDITUS ILLIS

ELABORATUM NEAPOLI

THEODORI MARCHIONIS DE NICOLAY SUMPTIBUS 1860

The gathering was incensed, and taking Christ forcibly they led him to the top of a hill outside the town. It was their intention "to throw him over it," but he passed through their midst miraculously and went on his way.

One of the smaller peaks in the western hills, the background of Nazareth, is shown as the place Christ eluded his plotters. It is "The Hill of the Precipice" or "The Mountain of the Leap." There is a stone altar and an apse cut into the rocky hill and, down below, the ruins of a monastery.

Another bit of pious tradition, drawn from the foregoing, states that Mary, having heard of her Son's misfortune, started to follow the irate citizens. Reaching the brow of the hill and seeing the Jews returning without Christ, her heart filled with fright, and, in swooning, the mountain melted to receive her body. Almost twelve centuries ago a monastery, "Our Lady of the Fear," was built on this spot. The present church used by Nubian Christians follows the ancient foundations.

Nazareth is mentioned in the post-Resurrection events and it is believed that the Risen Saviour did return to His hillside home sometime after Easter Sunday. Naturally his disciples would wish to extend the usual hospitality for which the East is noted. They prepared a meal for their Lord and the place of the gathering is called "The Church of Christ's Table." Under the dome of this chapel there is a large, hollowed-out block of limestone. Some pilgrims have gone so far as to maintain this was where Jesus multiplied the loaves, others as the place wherein He supped with the Apostles, while others state this is just part of an ancient Samaritan altar. The chapel is kept in repair by the Franciscans who hold services regularly.

A tour in the hills surrounding Nazareth revives many Scriptural memories. Springtime re-echoes the description of St. Matthew (vi, 29) "even Solomon in all his glory was not arrayed like one of

A marble altar in the crypt behind the site of the Annunciation

DEDERUNT ÆMILIUS HENNION, UXOR EJUS NATIQUE EORUM — ESTAIRES IN GALLIA ANNO 1890

these." The view from this elevation discloses the sweeping, fertile plains of Esdraelon; peaceful Carmel dipping gently into the Mediterranean blue on one end and marching along till it is lost in Samaria on the other; to the east are the peaks of Tabor, Little Hermon and the impressive white crown of Great Hermon, while to the south and north the sun spangles the Great Sea. The intervening miles blend into a composite beauty upon which the Master must have gazed, meditated and found as subject for sermon and parable. Our Blessed Lord's memories of Nazareth with its cruelty, ignorance and defeatism were softened by the recollection of his Mother, his home and the years of preparation for that day when He appeared among men and they—friend and foe, Jew and Gentile—would recognize "the kingdom of heaven is at hand." Mt. iii, 2.

WHEN MARY had accepted Gabriel's invitation the angel added a confirming word. Elizabeth, her cousin and wife of the priest Zachary, whose barren state had been a lifetime sorrow, was with child. In her advanced years she would soon be delivered because "no word is impossible to the Lord." Mary was startled and activity followed this revelation. Rising in haste she traveled over the hills to Ein Karim, home of her cousin. In her newly bestowed role, Mary could not remain passive, nor could she ignore a cause so urgent. Her love for God would be activated in service for her cousin.

"Blessed art thou among women, and blessed is the fruit of thy womb. How have I deserved to be thus visited by the Mother of my Lord?" (Lk. i, 42–43) asked Elizabeth, first to recognize "the Word was made flesh" and was dwelling amongst them. John wor-

*Friars climbing the long series of steps to the Church of the Visitation.
The Church of St. John the Baptist, in the background, is the
traditional site of the house of the High Priest, Zachary, father of St. John*

74

A Russian nun descending the hill from the Church of the Visitation. There is a Russian convent near this church

shiped too—for though still unborn he "leaped for joy" in the presence of His Maker. He who would become the forerunner of Jesus and declare that he was "the voice of one crying in the wilderness" yet unworthy "to untie the strap of his shoes" was the Saviour's first disciple, the only one who was ever verbally canonized. "God hath raised up no greater son of woman than John the Baptist." Mt. xi, 11.

John's integrity dedicated to making straight the way and preparing for Christ's coming would result in his beheading. Militant herald of the truth that Christ came on earth to teach, John would never permit a compromise and for this he fell—another victim of Herod's turpitude.

After Elizabeth's greeting, Mary, aware of her destiny as Mother of the Redeemer, takes upon her lips the exultant response, the lyrical cadences of the Magnificat. This is her biography, truth apprehended under poetic forms—long before that Truth became visible in the flesh. Her soul magnifies the Lord as her spirit rejoices in the redeeming Saviour; she exalts the wisdom of the Creator who has

The tower of the Church of St. John the Baptist

Close-up view of the Grotto of
St. John the Baptist, birthplace of the saint

The Grotto of St. John the Baptist at the eastern end of the church

Main altar in the church of St. John the Baptist.
There have been churches on this site since the 5th century

endowed his creature so that all nations shall call her blessed; she has become the pioneer of the race on its long journey home, where his mercy will extend from one generation to another so long as men will acknowledge his divinity.

Other women in old Israel had raised their voices in canticles, lauding the mercies of the Lord. There was Miriam, sister to Moses; Anna, mother of Samuel; Judith, deliverer of her people; but Mary surpassed them all. Her gratitude for the favor but recently bestowed, her consideration for the great things listed (the power of God not to be thwarted by little men, and mercy for everyone needing it) are gifts from the God still unseen but who has begun to live in His Mother, Mary.

The scene of this meeting and the dwelling of the priest, Zachary, which was also the birthplace of John the Baptist, did not disappear. In Constantine's reign there were churches built—enthusiastic memorials. Two houses, said to belong to Elizabeth's family, have been rich with traditional identification. The first, the regular home in Ein Karim, marks the miracles following on John's birth. When Zachary had been informed by an angel that his aged wife would have a child, he disbelieved the notice. For this doubt he "remained dumb" until it came time to name his son, John. His epitome of gratefulness is the "Benedictus," (Lk. i, 68) spoken after he regained his speech.

The church of St. John the Baptist is built against the side of the mountain. Bas-relief cover the sides of this underground chapel and the subjects shown are events in the life of the Precursor. An outstanding mosaic in the porch of the church with the inscription "Hail! Martyrs of God" commemorates some Greek monks who were murdered on this spot.

Recent excavations at St. John's have shown that a group of buildings existed here in Byzantine days, some of which were placed over pre-Christian edifices. Rock chambers, chapels, graves and the

mosaic floors of churches were among the findings of the diggers.

St. John's Church follows basilican lines, three aisles, side walls covered partially with blue tiles and the high altar dedicated to the saint. Beneath the nave is the Grotto where John the Baptist was born and where Zachary regained his speech.

On the small hill across the valley from St. John's, the Church of the Visitation stands out prominently with its richly colored mosaic façade depicting Mary arriving in Ein Karim. This work, designed by Biagetti, was made in the Vatican studios and when seen through the grille work of the surrounding enclosure ranks with the other outstanding mosaics in the rebuilt shrines.

The Visitation Church commemorates the meeting of Elizabeth with Mary and their exchange of felicitations. In this spot they both settled down to the daily ritual of living while waiting the nativity of St. John. The present church, constructed over several other churches built prior to the seventeenth century, was not completed until 1946. It is the work of Sig. Antonio Barluzzi, who is responsible for Gethsemane and Mt. Tabor churches. In the construction every remaining part of the former edifice, historical and religious, was preserved. In the crypt there is the well from which all pilgrims eagerly drink. Over the central door are the coats of arms of both the Franciscan Order and the Custody of the Holy Land; within, the floor is made of mosaic and marble and the ceiling is of Florentine design. The bronze doors, chandeliers and altar furnishings are from craftsmen in Rome.

The Shrine of the Visitation sits very attractively on the mountainside. In this atmosphere of solitude and natural beauty, it is not difficult to remember those whose roles were so important for Christ's coming and for man's redemption. The two Mothers—Mary who bore the Saviour, and Elizabeth who mothered Christ's Precursor John—seem to live again in this favored spot—a sanctuary to Motherhood at its highest. Thoughts rise toward heaven, like

An Arab tomb near the Church of the Visitation,
marked by a beautiful bronze head,
said to be that of St. John the Baptist, who was beheaded

The Church of the Visitation, which recalls Mary's Magnificat:
"My soul magnifies the Lord; my spirit has found joy in God, who is my Saviour,
because He has looked graciously upon the lowliness of His handmaid.
Behold, from this day forward all generations will count me blessed."
There was a church on this site from the 4th century
to the end of the Crusades. The Franciscans
have been there since 1679. The present upper church is modern

84

The new Church of the Visitation showing
altar and frescoes of Mary with choirs of angels

The Virgin's Fountain in Ein Karim

the tapering cedars, in a confession that "All things find in him their origin, their impulse, the centre of their being; to him be glory throughout all ages" (Rom. xi, 36) which is the motivation of the Franciscan builders.

BETHLEHEM

Although EIN KARIM is the first fruit of the Annunciation, the promises made to Mary in Nazareth came to literal fulfillment in Bethlehem. Who has not seen the pictures of the great bells in the City of David; the view of the steep, winding road leading into the square before the mayor's office and, in these later years, who has not heard the broadcasts coming directly from shrine and courtyard? Bethlehem, "House of Bread," was called Ephrata the Fruitful. The prophecy of Micheas mentions it honorably. "Bethlehem, Ephrata! least do they reckon thee among all the clans of Juda? Nay, it is from thee I look to find a prince that shall rule over Israel." Mich. v, 2.

The town is mentioned in the very first book of the Bible, Genesis (xxxv). Jacob and his wife Rachel were directed to a new dwelling in Hebron. Along the route Rachel, in giving birth to Benjamin, died. She "was buried on the way that leads to Ephrata (the same as Bethlehem). Over her tomb Jacob raised a monument . . . the Pillar of Rachel's tomb." Gen. xxxv, 19–20. The place has been venerated by Jews, Christians and Moslems as the exact site and there has never been any doubt or question concerning this shrine.

In 333, the Pilgrim of Bordeaux traveled to the Holy Land and described this monument and its location. Other details are mentioned nine centuries later, especially that a pyramid was formed there of twelve stones to symbolize the sons of Jacob and the twelve tribes of Israel. The Crusaders embellished the tomb but in a few centuries all the stones had disappeared, the building was walled up and the whole took on a mosque-like appearance. The white plastered walls have yellowed and flaked; names of pilgrims have been scratched in every possible part of the surface and the multicolored rags or threads are placed there to absorb the blessings and thus become treasured mementos.

Many stirring events took place in the little town of Bethlehem, the city of David and Booz and Ruth and the Saviour. Those who

The Cloister of St. Jerome at entrance to Church of St. Catherine in Bethlehem

88

came to visit the famed town throughout the ages took away many souvenirs when they returned home. The name, Bethlehem, must have held a fascination for it was repeated in the Lisbon town of Belem, in the sea-air base in Brazil, and there was the famous mental hospital in London, Our Lady in Bethlehem. That name became shortened, corrupted into "Bedlam," and the onetime asylum is now a museum for war relics.

Christ was born in Judea, rather than in Galilee, the home of his parents, because of an edict issued by the Roman Emperor that a census be taken of the kingdom. All men were to register in the place of their ancestors, thus Mary and Joseph, descended from the Davidic line, went up to Bethlehem. When they arrived Mary "brought forth a son . . . whom she laid in a manger, because there was no room for them in the inn." Lk. ii, 7. The fortunes of the world were changed by this birth, which has been inspiration for creative genius in every age. Regardless of the outpoured talents in an endeavor to gild the lily, the richness of the unadorned Gospel has never been surpassed. A tiny, helpless Babe is the Son of God—

Seminarians entering Parish Church for Christmas services in Bethlehem

89

90   *Clergy awaiting entry of the Latin Patriarch*
for the Christmas Procession in Bethlehem

older than eternity, younger than the day itself. Bethlehem becomes the gateway of the Kingdom of Heaven in that hour when He took growing life and asked only for that which was his by creation—the human heart. Over the fallow fields poured the heavenly comment, sung to startled shepherds, "Glory to God in high heaven and peace on earth to men that are God's friends." Lk. ii, 14. Peace, that blessing of Bethlehem, to be the possession of all who by selfless, surrendered lives come to this Child that they may have life eternal.

The birthplace of Christ is synonymous with Bethlehem. A great basilica stands over the spot, which is hardly perceptible from the street because of the surrounding monasteries. From earliest times this site, one of many caves cut into the rock, has been venerated as the place of the Nativity. A temple to the god Adonis was built here by a hostile emperor whose efforts to efface the memory of Christ only served as a more certain identification. Worship to the god disappeared as worship of the Infant Jesus gained adherents; thus there was no question about the right place. When St. Helena arrived the site was one of devotion. She transformed the cave into a great sanctuary and her son, Constantine, decorated the interior.

The approach to the basilica is over a wide paved court. Once there were three large bays; now there is only one, partially walled up and almost hidden by a sharp buttress. The door was sealed up to safeguard the sacred interior from profanation by any conqueror who might wish to enter on horseback. The present entry, just "a hole in the wall," might symbolize the Saviour of the world, whose humility deigned to select the little town of David for this great event.

The interior of the basilica is an unexpected contrast with the grim, fortress-like exterior. The rectangular nave is broken with four rows of tall pillars, forty in all, of dark-red marble. The white Corinthian capitals were set in place in the fourth century. During the years when the Crusaders ruled, the walls of this basilica were covered with gold mosaics on which half-length figures of the ancestors of Christ and the Seven Councils of the Church were depicted. In present work was finished by . . . Ephraim, under the rule of the the apse of the choir there is an inscription in Latin and Greek, "The Emperor . . . Comnenus, . . . in the time of the king of Jerusalem . . . and . . . the most holy Bishop of Jerusalem, my Lord, Raoul, in the year 1169."

At the far end of the nave, on a platform, is the sanctuary of the Greek Orthodox. Conspicuously hanging over the ornate choir screen are strings of ostrich eggs and the red covered lamps reminding one of a deserted ballroom. Beneath this raised altar two staircases lead into the rectangular crypt. The only light in this Grotto of the Nativity comes from fifty-three decorated lamps, dimly showing the marble walls and the heavy tapestry given by the French government. Where the stairs meet there is a semi-circular niche, partially hidden behind a gilded iron screen. This is the place of Christ's birth. Closer examination shows the traces of mosaics with Latin words. The grille-work about the altar is only opened in the early hours of the morning and is always guarded most zealously by a Greek monk. Below the altar table on the floor of marble, cleaned several times a week by Armenian and Greek clergy exclusively, there is a silver star around which is the dedication, "Here Jesus Christ was born of the Virgin Mary." This is the spot to which the Prince of Peace came, this is where Christmas originated. The star has had one misfortune—in 1847 it disappeared. In the long history of Palestine many claimants for the Holy Places have appeared, despite unchallenged records and indisputable history. So in Bethlehem, as in the Holy Sepulchre and Calvary, other religious sects appear and conduct their services not always without asperity and quarrels. The casual visitor, learning of this for the first time, or witnessing such strident competition in the service of God, will draw very hasty conclusions which will appear later in

Christmas procession, showing Bethlehem in the background

Christmas procession nearing the entrance to Church

written accounts. But, back to the Star of Bethlehem. More than five years the negotiations continued, only to be hampered by the intrigues of the Russian ambassador. At length a settlement was made and the Greek Orthodox clergy were obliged to restore and affix the star as it is seen today. There is another story told that the theft of one of the silver nails holding the Star was the indirect cause of the Crimean War.

Not more than four steps away there are two small oratories. The smaller, and nearer to the floor, is the Altar of the Manger which was the feeding trough for beasts and in which Mary placed her newborn Son. This was his first throne when the shepherds came

94

to adore Him. Their presence, summoned by angels to the Midnight Cave, incorporated the worth and dignity of laborers into the Christian code of ethics. Opposite the Manger is an elaborate marble table to honor the Magi, those Eastern Kings, who followed the guiding Star to Bethlehem. The remembrance of this visit was observed here in the fourth century. Another tradition marks this as the place of Christ's circumcision, when He was given the name Jesus.

There are many hollowed-out recesses in the passages under the church, usually chapels named to honor incidents associated with the Divine Infant. There is the Chapel of the Holy Innocents opened only on December 28, when the cruel deed of Herod is liturgically remembered; St. Joseph's Chapel where the angel advised him to flee into Egypt; the oratory of St. Jerome where he worked on the translation of the Bible; and the chapels named for his followers, Sts. Paula and Eustochium. Above the stairs and to the west is the parish church of Bethlehem, dedicated to St. Catherine of Alexandria. The Franciscan personnel of this monastery go in procession every evening to the Grotto and other shrines where prayers are made for enduring peace among nations.

Entrance to the Church of the Nativity

95

The Roman Catholic Church was established by Christ when he commissioned Peter to be its first leader. After Peter established himself in Rome, the Apostle James, the Just, was named to govern the growing colony of devout souls in Jerusalem. The expansion of the Church was limited, persecutions frequent and fear filled all Christians in the first four centuries of the era. Then came St. Helena and a marked improvement was noticed. During this period the representative leader of the Church came to be known by the title Patriarch. Any sanguine hopes that may have filled the followers of Christ were thwarted with the spread of Islam and it was not until after the capture of Jerusalem in 1099 by the Crusaders that the Patriarchate was to flourish. Two hundred years of history saw the Latin kingdom in Jerusalem and the Church interwoven. The fall of Acre, the dispersal of the Franks, and the victories of the Moslems meant the end of Patriarchal jurisdiction. The title was never permitted to fall into disuse but it was given, *honoris causa*, to outstanding churchmen. Little more than a century ago, 1847, it came into active use and Jerusalem again had a church leader, a Patriarch. There have been six prelates so named since that re-establishment, of whom the present, Patriarch Albert Gori, came to the honor in the Holy Year of 1950. Previous to this elevation, Monsignor Gori had been Custos of the Holy Land, i.e., Superior of all the Franciscan missionaries in Syria, Lebanon, Palestine, Israel, Jordan, Cyprus and Egypt.

What the Pope is in Rome, so are the several Patriarchs, Greeks, Armenian, Syrian and Coptic, considered by their sects; and wherever they participate in religious ceremonies there is always a concourse of adherents, additional protocol and indications of filial esteem. In Bethlehem, on the eve of Christmas, the Latin commemoration of December 24, His Beatitude the Latin Patriarch comes with a resplendent entourage to make "The Solemn Entry" into the city. Everything is festive; the designs on the native costumes repeat

Priests and nuns praying before the Manger on Christmas

97

The Franciscan parish priest distributing Communion
near the Manger in the crypt of the Church of the Nativity

Figure of the Christ Child
in the Crypt beneath
the Church of the Nativity

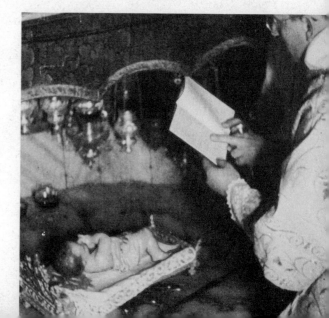

the red of tarboosh and flaming geraniums; the white, sedate, high headdresses of the Christian matrons stir the memory to their Crusader ancestry who left this bit of regal dress in the distant land.

After midday the inclined street leading up to the basilica is crowded with eager citizens. Suddenly a bearded cleric charges into the road. Riding astride a white horse, he holds up a standard topped with the cross. This is the signal that the Patriarch has arrived. The people become enthusiastically vocal, a haphazard procession begins, several boys' bands do their best to make the brass heard and a group of seminarians attempt hymns for the occasion. There is a jovial air of religious unrestraint. Everyone is happy, especially the omnipresent vendors of sticky sweetmeats and trays of colored nuts. Order is restored only when the Patriarch stoops to enter the little door of the basilica and make his way to the throne in St. Catherine's Church. The clergy, diplomats and civic representatives are formally presented and Vespers, the ancient evensong of the Catholic Church, is solemnly chanted. The many-tongued bells ring out when the service is over, repeating again the "Good news . . . for the whole people" that "a Saviour has been born for you, the Lord Christ Himself." Lk. ii, 10–11. Amid the swirls of fragrant incense the church empties, friends gather in the little streets, merchants vie for trade, exerting more than usual blandishment—sometimes even a persuasive coercion. And over the whole town comes a stillness, noticeable after the surcharged activity of the morning.

The several observances of Christmas and Easter are other perplexing things about the Holy Land. The calendar introduced by Julius Caesar, forty-six years before the birth of Christ, contained errors of calculation. There were ten days extra to be eliminated and an arrangement was so devised that there would be no recurrence of this mistake in the future. Pope Gregory XIII in 1582 had the corrections made; ten days were dropped in that year and every fourth year an extra day was added. The newly introduced system bears the name of this pope, Gregorian. At first only the Catholic nations accepted the reform, later it was adopted by other countries. But the Eastern Orthodox Churches, following the Greek nation, did not comply with the changes and they still observe, for liturgical reckoning, the Julian calendar. Thus, the Orthodox Christmas is always on the sixth of January when the Latins are celebrating Little Christmas, or the Epiphany.

On Christmas Eve the bells ring out around ten and the basilica

Typical camel riders on the desert, similar to lands passed by the Holy Family en route to Egypt

8 Januarii 1950

A stained-glass window — the Flight into Egypt
— Franciscan Hospice, Bethlehem

Christmas procession outside the Basilica of the Nativity

begins to fill up again for the Midnight Mass. An inflexible protocol, formerly entrusted to the French, assigns the seating arrangement for this gathering. Frequently there will be mild disputes concerning places but the master of ceremonies has seen such feasts come and go, and with typical Oriental charm he pleases or placates the most vociferous disputant.

When the Patriarch, attired in rich robes and the jeweled mitre, ascends the throne, the Mass commences. From the glitter of gold on uniforms, to the flashes of camera bulbs and the measured movement of those assisting in the sanctuary, to the blended voices of soaring chant, everything harmonizes to make this an unforgettable occasion. Christmas is a special day for Franciscans. St. Francis, lover of all creation and close follower of Jesus, popularized devotion to the crèche and left a legacy of tenderness for the Infant Saviour.

When the Mass is over there is another procession through the church and down into the Grotto of the Nativity. The Patriarch, carrying on a silken cushion a lifelike carved image of the Bambino, arrives in the crypt, where the figure is placed on the Star under the altar. The Gospel which relates the birth of Christ is sung and the figure is taken from one altar, the Nativity, to be placed amid the straw of the Manger. Christmas has officially begun. Other services will follow in this spot until late afternoon and the register of those who offer Masses looks like a convention of nations. Sunrise brings the scheduled visits to the Patriarch, greetings to be exchanged with the heads of religious orders and the civilian government, and then the home festivities.

On the feast of the Epiphany, Twelfth Night or Little Christmas, the other rites, Greeks, Armenians, Copts and Syrians, will repeat this day which recalls heaven stooping down to earth.

Bethlehem has been among the famed places of pilgrimage down the centuries. The little town where Christ took our growth upon

Himself and made humanity a link in the eternal plan, is a kindly place. There lingers about the small houses and streets a convincing serenity, despite shattered buildings and barbed wire enclosures. Once Bethlehem had no room for God, today it has made room for many refugee Arabs who have come to depend on the religious groups for livelihood, shelter and clothing.

From the terrace of the Casa Nova or Guest House adjoining St. Catherine's, the panorama is refreshing. Down below is the paved courtyard, and beyond, the grim, grayish stone buildings are spotted with lichens and newly repaired masonry. Side by side with cross and dome are the slender minarets and sprawling dwellings. To the west are tiny patches of cultivation, vineyards and scattered boulders, tossed about as though giants had been at play. Farther away the wrinkled ridges of Moab, the mountains of Jordan just beyond the Dead Sea, gleam with an iridescence in the late morning sunshine. And down in an olive grove the black tents of Bedouins have appeared since yesterday. Somewhere a donkey protests, smoke rises from houses and the quiet returns. Taking a last look over Bethlehem one remembers that, "there are sermons in stones, books in the running brooks and good in everything"—especially in Bethlehem.

Almost any day in the year small gatherings of women, not only Christian but Moslem, are seen entering and leaving a chapel in the street east of the Basilica of the Nativity. This shrine has been built, in the usual way, over a rock grotto and is called in Arabic, "The Grotto of Lady Mary," or "The Milk Grotto." The Virgin Mary with her child and husband stopped in this spot while making the journey to Egypt. The prayers of many have been offered here. Judging from the rich collection of jewels heaped on the statue of Mother Mary, her response has been prompt and extensive. Records attest that a series of churches were built in this place long before the coming of the Franks. The decorations within rival the multicolored flowers that enliven the walled garden.

Archbishop Gustavo Testa, Apostolic Delegate, officiating at Midnight Mass in Bethlehem, Christmas Eve; to the left, Monsignor Thomas J. McMahon, President of the Pontifical Mission

OT TOO FAR DISTANT from the center of Bethlehem extends a fertile strip of land, the Field of Booz. In this locality Ruth, the Moabite woman, met her husband Booz. Obed, ancestor of David, was their son. In these fields the "Glory to God in the highest" was first sung to the surprised shepherds by the angelic heralds. The Christians in the village have much pride in pointing out ruins of early churches to substantiate the claim. A few months ago a new church was built to care for the increased population.

The road from Bethlehem passes through Jerusalem and on to Nazareth, the setting of Christ's hidden years. In the seclusion of the hills our Saviour emerged into manhood. Leaving his home he retired into the desert to preface the active years with prayer and fasting. The conclusion of the vigil was the ordeal of temptations mentioned by the sacred writers. The Mountain of Quarantine near Jericho is pointed out as the likely place for such an experience. The rocks are perforated with many caves ideal for contemplation and retirement. Atop the mountain is the place where Christ was taken by the devil to be shown the kingdoms of the world and offered such in exchange for the Saviour's submission. Satan, after repeated re-proofs, was completely routed and angels came to minister to Christ. (Mt. iv, 1–11.) Tradition has made this a favorite, though arduous, place of devotion.

After the temptations, the Master returned to Galilee, "for the kingdom of God was at hand," and his mission began. His activities, crowded into less than three years, make an unusual catalog. Mira-

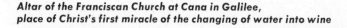

Altar of the Franciscan Church at Cana in Galilee,
place of Christ's first miracle of the changing of water into wine

The Tomb of Lazarus in Bethany

Another view of the Tomb of Lazarus

cles of many kinds, teaching, preaching, establishing his church, training the men he had selected as disciples, listening to the outcasts, scattering his divine largess—the entire mission years are presented with that laconic observation, "He went about doing good." St. John, on the contrary, becomes graphic. "There are many other miracles Jesus did in the presence of his disciples, which are not written in this book; so much has been written down, that you may learn to believe Jesus is the Christ, and so believing find life through his name." Jo. xx, 31.

Cana, a short distance from Nazareth, was the village in which the Master chose to assume his public ministry. The miracle that took place at the wedding is too well known for any but a passing reference. But the significance is not just a setting for Christ's generosity—it is the first time specific proof of His divinity was given to a group. Moreover, this manifestation took place only after his Mother had made known the shortage of wine and had advised the servants, "Do whatever he tells you." Jo. ii, 1–11.

The village, home of Nathaniel, is but a collection of squalid hovels for the poor villagers. There is a touch of the oasis about the settlement with its few olives, vines, apricots and hedges of prickly cactus. A red-and-white church is companion with the dilapidated mosque. In the crypt of the church there are some water jugs which may or may not be the kind used for weddings.

Many miles farther south, Bethany, the home of Mary, Martha and their brother Lazarus, was another village that often witnessed the power of the Son of God. In this locality, about two miles from Jerusalem, our Divine Lord epitomized the purpose of creation, "But only one thing is necessary" Lk. x, 38–42; in the house of Simon the leper He was anointed by Mary when the valuable ointment was poured upon his feet as a preparation for his burial (Jo. xii, 1–10); from thence He sent his disciples to find the colt for the ride into Jerusalem on Palm Sunday (Lk. xix, 29–44); and on the out-

110

*Mount Tabor, the "Holy Mountain," scene of the Transfiguration of Christ.
In the foreground lies the fertile Plain of Esdraelon*

skirts of the town He met the grief-stricken sisters before raising
Lazarus from the dead. Martha, on this occasion, so ably professed
her faith, "I have learned to believe thou art the Christ . . . the
Son of the living God; it is for thy coming the world has waited."
Jo. xi, 1–44.

Turning north again to Nazareth, many miles distant, we see the
stately peak of Mount Tabor rise from the western end of the plain
of Esdraelon to almost 2,000 feet above the Mediterranean. Because
of its graceful shape, the abundant vegetation and the splendor of
the panorama, it stands out like "a majestic altar that the Creator has

Gate of the Wind, Mt. Tabor. Road leads to the Basilica of the Transfiguration

The Basilica of the Transfiguration, completed in 1924.
Franciscan monastery in the foreground

**Greek church of St. Elias with hills sloping from
Mt. Tabor to the Sea of Galilee**

114

built Himself, great among all the mountains of the country." A roadway leading to the top seems like a zigzagging golden thread in the distance. In the ninth century a flight of 4,340 steps made it possible for pilgrims to get to the summit. This was once a frontier for Israel and is known to the Arabs as Jebel el Tour, the Holy Mountain. On its slopes Deborra, the Prophetess ruler of Israel, called Barac to battle the hosts of Sisara. The gratitude of the Jews for the successful outcome of this conflict is enshrined in the Canticle of Debbora (Jud. v).

Mount Tabor was always considered holy by the Jewish tribes, and it was the theme of poetic comparisons used by the Prophets (Jer. xlvi, 18). Although not mentioned by name in the Gospel it has been a venerable tradition that this was the mountain where Christ took Peter, James and John to be transfigured. Origen, who lived from 185–254, says, "Tabor is the mountain of Galilee on which Christ was transfigured," and to this many other witnesses might be added.

Mount Tabor had a church on its crown as early as the fourth century and in the sixth there were three churches on the spot where Peter had exclaimed in his eagerness, "Lord, it is well that we should be here . . . let us make three arbors in this place, one for thee, one for Moses and one for Elias." Mt. xvii, 1–8.

In the year 1101 Mount Tabor was given over to the care of the Benedictine Monks who were succeeded by the Hospitalers of St. John in 1255. The Egyptian army destroyed the sacred edifices in 1263 and they remained in ruins until 1920. Of interest to Americans is the "American Vow" made in 1888 to rebuild the ancient basilica by the first pilgrimage from their country. At that time the Turkish Government refused but in 1919 the cornerstone was laid amid the ancient ruins and the walls began to rise over the foundations. The official dedication came in the spring of 1924. During the building the stone was quarried and cut to size on the property and

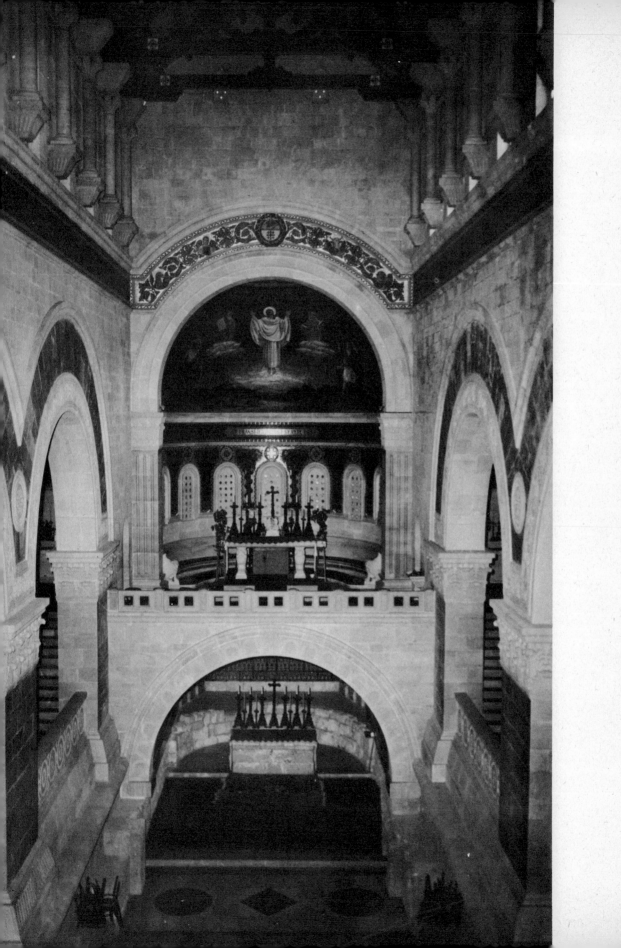

ET TRANSFIGVRATVS EST ANTE EOS

The Transfiguration mosaic, showing Christ surrounded by
Peter, James and John with Moses and Elias in the background

The Nave of the Church of the Transfiguration.
The striking figure of Christ dominates the interior

117

the water was brought in from the little town of Endor, famous in the Bible for its witch.

Towering above the verdant slope the sturdy white stone walls of the basilica are majestic and impressive and can be seen for miles away. Rose-tinted in the dawn, mellow and mystic by moonlight, this Shrine is the most outstanding in all the country of Palestine. In every detail it does honor to Christ, transfigured and identified on this height, as "My beloved Son; to him, then, listen." Lk. ix, 35.

The façade of the basilica is broken with a richly sculptured arch resting on two slender towers which rise over the old chapels dedicated to Moses and Elias, Peter's wish now realized. The magnificent triple nave is divided by pilasters connected with arches. Above these are a series of alabaster windows and colonnettes supporting the rafters, left exposed to view and the alabaster forming the roof. The whole interior is so constructed that the entire edifice can be seen at a single glance from the narthex. The crypt still preserves the ancient walls and the venerable altar discovered during excavation. The apse contains the resplendent mosaic scenes of the Transfiguration, while the vault is decorated with mosaics representing incidents from the life of Christ. The jeweled double peacock window in the crypt and the bronze statues, as well as the gleaming pavement, endow this memorial with the glory of religious artistry.

The actual construction and art work were planned by Antonio and Giulio Barluzzi; the mosaics are from the Vatican workshops.

As the sun shines upon this basilica that owes its erection to the munificence of the Catholics of the United States, visitors who come can exclaim with St. Peter, "Lord, it is well for us to be here."

On the plateau there are ruins of a twelfth-century Benedictine Abbey, a Saracen fortress and a rebuilt Greek Orthodox Church dedicated to St. Elias. A few steps away there is shown the cave where Melchisedech, contemporary of Abraham, dwelt. Where the little road comes up the side of the mountain it crosses under a

*Crypt in the Basilica of the Transfiguration with
"jeweled double peacock window" and mosaics of adoring angels*

gate appropriately called "The Gate of the Winds." Nearby is another small chapel marking the place where Christ cautioned his disciples, "Do not tell anybody of what you have seen until the Son of Man has risen from the dead." Mt. xvii, 9.

Another expanse of land may be seen from the terrace of the rambling, comfortable guest house. Two villages, well known from

119

The altar in one of the towers of the Church,
showing Elias with the fire of the Lord consuming his sacrifice

Within the other tower, showing Moses with the Tablets of the Law

122 *The Sea of Galilee from the Mount of the Beatitudes,
where Christ preached the Sermon on the Mount*

123

the biblical narrative, are in the distance, Nain and Endor. Nain or Naim, is set comfortably in the lowlands of Little Hermon and is mentioned both in the Talmud and the Bible. The miracle performed by Jesus, raising from death the only son of a poor widow, gave to the village its lasting distinction and set forth again the compassion of Him who came "so that they may have life and have it more abundantly." Jo. x, 10. There are rock tomb ruins, a seldom used chapel and a plentiful spring to make this a desirable settlement for farming folk.

Endor, the other village, became renowned when Saul, Israel's leader, visited the resident fortuneteller. Breaking his pledges made to God, he demanded that the witch call up the spirit of Samuel in order to have advance information concerning the morrow's battle. The good news anticipated was quite the reverse. Saul's chagrin may be imagined when he was told that all had forsaken him, he and his sons would die on the field the next day and the kingdom would be taken over by David.

The present village is built on the remains of a volcanic mountain. It has the usual burial caves, grain pits and cisterns and a useful little spring. Apart from the story of the Witch of Endor it is but another settlement of people struggling for a livelihood.

Westward from Tabor the road winds and begins a steady descent. Off to one side rises the phenomena of twin peaks, the Horns of Hattin. Among the foothills and on the plain the most decisive battle of the Crusader armies was waged July 4, 1187. The army of Saladin routed the forces of Raymond, Count of Tripoli, in what was the bloodiest conflict of the Frankish occupation. The Knights had held this land for about a century and lost it in less than two days. All that Europe had poured into the Crusade movement was lost that day when the Christian armies went down before Islam. One after another of the Christian posts, cities, garrisons and institutions were swept clean of anything relating to the Saviour.

The altar of the Shrine of the Beatitudes,
situated on the northwestern shore of the Sea of Galilee

Jerusalem held out for a week and then surrendered. By October of that year every Knight and Hospitaler who had not escaped was vanquished or were given into slavery. The Crusade had failed—the True Cross was dragged through the streets of Damascus and over the land came Moslem domination, giving no quarter to any but the Sons of the Prophet. Two centuries of Latin legislation were gone forever.

As the dipping highway comes closer to the Sea of Galilee, farming methods improve, the grass is greener, and trees more plentiful. After hours of looking on brown hills and scorched, waterless valleys this is a refreshing change. Tiberias, the city founded by Herod, is at the end of the highway. In the time of Christ this was one in a chain of nine cities that ringed the sea. Today it is the sole reminder of a thriving period of urban progress.

The old section of Tiberias looks like a deserted village with broken down walls, two almost destroyed mosques, the Mosque of the Sea and the Mosque of the Sand, and the ancient synagogue. The thermal springs about which much of the luxurious Herodian life centered are still in use. In all the squalor and destruction brought about by war it is difficult to remember this great city of marble villas, colonnades and the opulence Christ saw on his visits. In the second and third centuries of the Christian era, the seat of the Jewish Sanhedrin, the birthplace of the Talmud and the codification and interpretation of the Mosaic laws, was in Tiberias. The accepted system of vocalization still used for reading the Hebrew scriptures comes from that city too.

The city is situated about seven hundred feet below sea level and fronts the lake. The residential section has spread into the newer development which is strictly Jewish. Tombs of such eminent scholars as Rabbi Meir, a Talmudist; Rabbi Akiba and Maimonides the philosopher are near the hot springs. The history of Tiberias is one of Jewish, Christian and Moslem occupancy. When Jerusalem fell to the Duke Godfrey he gave the entire province of Galilee to Tancred, who, like Herod, made this city his capital. The little church with an apse resembling a ship's keel is all that remains of the Crusader's stay. Today Tiberias is the center of extensive Jewish colonization where much has been accomplished through modern farming methods.

Tiberias will always be associated with the calling of Peter, Andrew, James and John to become Apostles, "Come and follow me; and I will make you into fishers of men" (Mt. iv, 19) and with that post-Resurrection confession of Peter that Christ was the "Son of the living God."

Some of the villages scattered around the lakeside carry one back to the Galilean ministry. There is the present Magdal, ancient Magdala, a squalid place of mud hovels and desperately poor Arabs. This is the village of the beautiful Mary whose meeting with Jesus

Floor mosaic representing Hope, in the Shrine of the Beatitudes

128 *The site of Capharnaum on the Sea of Galilee,
where Christ lived and taught*

will ever be encouraging for those who approach the forgiving Saviour. Ruins of a church are still shown, but even these seem to have been stripped of all reverence.

Tabigah, said to be the spot from which Jesus sat in the gunwale of a boat and discoursed to the crowds, has part of a church built to commemorate the miraculous feeding of the five thousand. Bethsaida, on the opposite shore of the lake, was in Christ's time, as the name implies, a fishing village—"The House of Fishing." Our Saviour came here often but the continual ingratitude of the people who had been sharers and witnesses of so many wonders brought the reminder, "Woe to thee, Bethsaida! Tyre and Sidon would have repented long ago, humbling themselves . . . if the miracles done in you had been done there instead." Lk. x, 13–14.

The traditional site where Christ preached some of his most encouraging sermons is a small knoll commanding a broad expanse of the shimmering lake, the Mount of the Beatitudes. In this natural pulpit the Great Teacher gave his listeners that unique declaration of independence, the Eight Beatitudes—a code both disciplinary and transforming. "I have a new commandment to give you," (Jo. xiii, 34) stated the Saviour, who then proceeded to outline the blessings which come on man's pattern of behavior when motivated by fellowship with Him. The new commandments show the purposeful and enriching results attendant on being poor in spirit, merciful, patient, clean of heart, bent on maintaining concord and conscious of that kinship which should unite all mankind. The church commemorating this well-known sermon is built on the hillock and follows earlier octagonal lines.

Capharnaum, on the northwest shore of Tiberias, was a thriving town in the time of Christ. Situated between the kingdoms of Herod and Philip, it was a center for fishing and commerce and had its own custom house. The Arabic name, Tell Hum, is a corruption of Kaphar Nahum, the village of Nahum derived from a Rabbi Nahum

129

who was buried near the place. Like Nazareth, the New Testament alone mentions the city abounding with so many associations, and it was called by Jesus "his own city." Mt. ix, 1.

After the miracle in Cana, our Blessed Lord, his mother and the disciples came to Capharnaum which became an important center of missionary activity and the setting for so many of his utterances. Not only was his divinity made manifest here but it was the scene of oft-repeated tendernesses. In Capharnaum, Levi, later Matthew, was called from his tax-collecting table; the daughter of Jairus the ruler was raised from death; the paralytic was given sound health as was the woman who touched the fringe of his garment. To this city came

Ancient aqueduct north of Haifa. This pre-Christian structure carried water from Lebanon down the entire coast of Palestine

Peter, his brother Andrew; the Sons of Thunder, James and John; and a multitude of sick people, among them Peter's mother-in-law; as well as demoniacs and lepers to experience the healing power of the Son of God, who offered this credential in the synagogue, "It is I who am the bread of life; he who comes to me will never be hungry, he who has faith in me will never know thirst." Jo. vi, 35.

Jealous of Christ's increasing popularity and miraculous endowments, the Pharisees stirred up the people to openly refuse the faith that was offered them. Another malediction was delivered, "Thou Capharnaum . . . shalt be brought low as hell." Lk. x, 15. This rejection saw the city sink into almost nothingness before the first century ended. It has never recaptured its importance or prosperity and today it is only a scattered village, its synagogue but a heap of stones around the shore. Much of that stone, white limestone, has disappeared but with what remains some reconstruction has been started. There are some who claim this was the place where Christ taught, others maintain it was the setting for Paul's trenchant discourses, while others place it as a second-century seat of worship. Regardless of what the age really is, the rebuilt portion shows it was large and very ornate. The decorative pieces are carved with rosettes, grapes, leaves, Solomon's seal, the shield of David, pomegranates, seven branch candlesticks and two interesting inscriptions, the names of those who contributed toward the building.

The years of Christ's public activity passed quickly and it was "from that time onwards Jesus began to make it known to his disciples that he must go up to Jerusalem, and there . . . be put to death, and rise again on the third day." Mt. xvi, 21. Simon Peter would strive to have Christ remain in the relative security of the country but once again he had to be taught "the man who tries to save his life shall lose it; it is the man who loses his life for my sake that will secure it." Mt. xvi, 25.

JERUSALEM AND ENVIRONS

To go up to Jerusalem, "a city set upon a hill that cannot be hid," from the rural calm of Galilee resembles any change from country to city. There is a quicker pace, a perceptible eagerness about the people and traffic jogs along noisily over streets. Nowhere do we find words that have become so poignantly true—"He who would travel to the Indies must take with him the wealth of the Indies." Every tourist and pilgrim to the Holy Land should keep those words in mind. In "the good old days" throngs came to Jerusalem, having visited great cities on the Continent and the Mediterranean countries. Upon arriving, and meeting with a few discomforts, the exasperating norm was repeated too often, "Back home, we; In Paris, or Madrid, or Venice, . . ." Facts being what they are, there are some features of the Holy Land that should not be glossed over, nor should they be ridiculed as some fault of the country. Judean hills are bleak and without growth except in the springtime. After the winter rains not even the verdant deserts of Arizona can offer more luxuriant flora than these same hillocks carpeted with the red anemone, the wild cyclamen, the new shoots of olive and vine. There are beggars of every age and description, and they do whine and persist in being irritating; a sense of punctuality is negligible; standards of living are considerably behind the West and many conveniences that we regard as indispensable are, in Palestine, only for the very wealthy. But guests never do behave badly in someone else's house.

Poor Jerusalem does want to be friendly to all comers. There is no pretense, nothing is discreetly hidden lest it offend the gimlet gaze of the critical. About the Holy City there is a take-it-or-leave-it

No Man's Land between Israeli Jerusalem (left) and Arab Jerusalem (right) near Mandelbaum Gate at frontier

attitude. The Old City has tried to become modernized, but herculean difficulties stand in the way of such civic improvement. Families will not concede readily to have their cubby holes destroyed; merchants have not the long-ranged vision to see additional gains in open shops and widened streets; and the people, in general, are loath to have the relics of their forebears disappear in what today may be changed or owned by another tomorrow.

Coming to Jerusalem, we recall the words, "My thoughts are not your thoughts: nor your ways my ways." Isai. lv, 8. Whatever road leads to the city affords a view that is inspiring. Upon the brow of a hill the medieval city is perched and encircled with massive walls that dip sometimes and seem to disappear in other places. Parapets rise with the clarity of an etching and over the bulwark peep the pinnacles, spires, domes and towers, some of them recognizable from photographs. This is the city that has been besieged by the armies of the Hebrews, Assyrians, Babylonians, Egyptians, Greeks, Romans, Persians, Saracens, French and English. Small wonder Jerusalem has been called "the city of magnificent differences" when each conquoror left some memorial of his occupation.

In the Wall surrounding the city there are a number of gates giving entry to some of the older parts of the town. The usual entrance is through the busy Jaffa Gate, "Gate of the Friend," which goes into David Street and leads out toward Bethlehem and Hebron. The Damascus Gate, called the Gate of Victory because the traditions of victory were preserved here, is probably on the site of the Northern Gate in existence at the time of Christ. The Gate of St. Stephen, called by the Moslem "Lady Mary's Gate," is the only one opening on the Cedron Valley and to the Virgin's Tomb. It corresponds to the ancient gate Probatica or the Sheep Gate and through this opening the Palm Sunday procession passes. The other gates have less importance. In fact they are not often mentioned to visitors, who have so many other points of interest to inspect.

134

*Most Rev. Albert Gori, O.F.M., Latin Patriarch of Jerusalem,
officiating at the Holy Sepulchre on Easter Sunday*

135

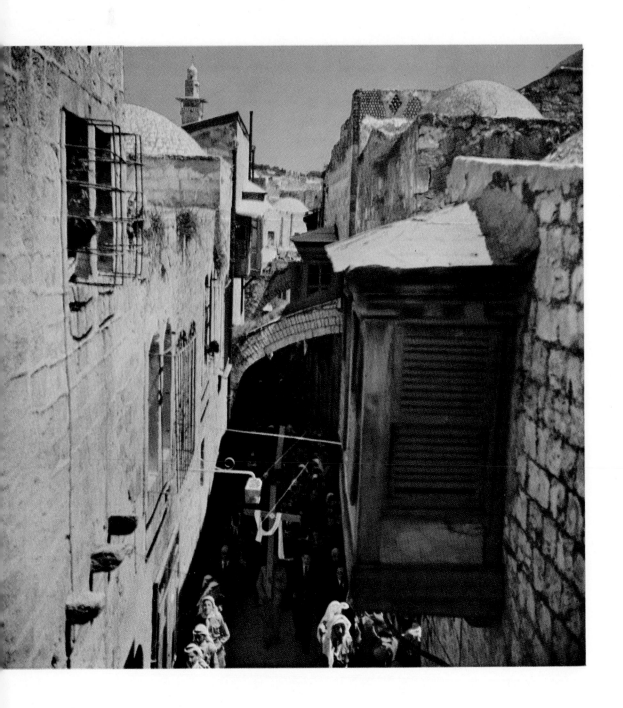

*Procession on the Via Dolorosa, the Way of the Cross,
going from the site of Pilate's Court to Calvary*

Looking through the Jaffa Gate toward the New City of Jerusalem with King David Hotel and tower of the YMCA in background

Jerusalem panorama. Top left, Hadassah hospital; top center, Augusta Victoria hospital; top right, the Mount of Olives. In the foreground is a section of the old wall. The Dome of the Rock is in left center

Entrance to the Tower of David in the Old City

Another view of the Tower of David

141

Alongside the Jaffa Gate is the Citadel, a fortress with five towers considered to be on the site of Herod's palace. It has been called by Christians the Tower of David. Little remains now of former construction except the foundation. Passing through the Gate into the Old City, one sees little slits in the Wall through which the green fields far below appear, or the dry valley of Cedron, or a steep incline topped with a medieval tower. The fetid lanes crowded with bazaars and shops displaying assorted wares—small, ill-lighted cubicles where the odors of spices and fish commingle; where groceries and carcasses are fully exposed to dust and rain; where the steady tapping of hammers means the cobblers are fashioning the turned-up slippers of colored leathers; where lintels and doorposts are draped with figs, grapes and viscera of freshly killed sheep; where the desk of the professional letter writer is seen side by side with fennel, okra and pomegranate. The sharp command to move over hurls from the camel driver as his lordly beast moves along without yielding an inch and the loaded basket panniers brush the shoppers. Sugar cane, sunflowers seeds and nuts replace chewing gum for those who find no diversion in the pungent Turkish cigarettes. Various are the cries of roving vendors dispensing beverages, seeking employment or just making themselves heard above the din.

The places which have been associated with Christ in and around Jerusalem will be the chief concern for Christian visitors. Many of the events in the life of the Master have been brought together and grouped in liturgical services held the week before Easter. The public activity of Jesus had angered the Pharisees and the rabbis. His preaching, miracles and very life were so reactionary that they resolved something had to be done. He had aroused the populace with the accent on justice, love and mercy; they were made aware of the venal demands of the Temple custodians, and his dicta concerning the true meaning of life as a spiritual and eternal endowment caused a dissatisfaction in those who thought only of the temporal

The Latin Patriarch of Jerusalem greets the Consular Corps on Easter Sunday. The painting on the wall shows the Pope receiving Knights of the Holy Sepulchre

A Rev. Canon in the Latin Patriarchate of Jerusalem

and tangible. Accordingly, when Jesus arrived in Bethany to stay with Mary and Martha, six days before the Passover of the Jews (Jo. xii, 1), his enemies saw the victim coming closer to the trap.

Sunday morning came and Jesus decided to visit the Holy City. As he drew near the gates the crowd became exuberant; they recognized the Wonder Worker—perhaps some of them had been beneficiaries—and voice echoed voice in proclaiming, "Hosanna, blessed is he who comes in the name of the Lord, blessed is the king of Israel." Jo. xii, 13.

The spectacle accorded returning heroes is a familiar one—the air white with confetti and torn paper swirling above the streets. That spring morning must have been one when genuine emotion welled from grateful hearts. The people spread their multicolored

Palm Sunday Procession from the Church of Bethphage

145

cloaks over the dusty way, plucked the long fronds from the date palms and tossed bunches of flowers as enthusiasm rose. His plotting enemies were aghast; that such things could take place—in the very shadow of the Temple—was carrying things a bit too far. It was scandalous enough that the rural communities in Galilee should run after this Nazarene, but, "Look, the whole world has turned aside to follow him." Jo. xii, 19. Hatred was fanned more and more— and Christ's enemies became more resolute than ever that some ruse must be found to seize this victim of their passion.

The Palm Procession crossed over the Mount of Olives and turned

Palm Sunday Procession passing through St. Stephen's Gate

Auxiliary Bishop Gelat in the Palm Sunday Procession

into the city close by the Temple. The shouts of the crowds continued and reached into the byways. To Jew and Gentile, Christ reiterated his purpose in coming to earth, that the time was coming to an end and that not only would He suffer but the little flock would fare no better and would be dispersed. Despite what would come there would be blessings on the world because of his sacrifice. "Yes, if only I am lifted up from the earth, I will attract all men to myself. (In saying this, He prophesied the death He was to die," Jo. xii, 32–33). Night shadows were falling as he continued to speak that first Palm Sunday (Mk. xi, 11) and with the Apostles he returned to Bethany.

Christ's triumphant entry into the Holy City is an annual cele-

148

Church dignitaries including
the Latin Patriarch (center),
Auxiliary Bishop (left) and
Most Rev. Hyacinth Faccio, O.F.M.,
Custos of the Holy Land (right),
in Palm Sunday procession

149

bration on Palm Sunday. Step by step the route follows the Saviour from Bethphage into St. Stephen's Gate, up to the Crusader's Church, St. Anne's. There is a white donkey, the guard of honor ornately accoutered; Jerusalem Boy Scouts; a marshal, officious and often perplexed; communities of priests and sisters—all bearing palm branches. Last in line is the resplendent Patriarch of Jerusalem flanked by his attendants. The crowd moves with reverence singing hymns, reciting psalms and litanies, and bearing in mind the significance Holy Week has for all Catholics. In St. Anne's there is Benediction with the crowd kneeling devoutly.

Thursday in Holy Week is the next occasion for public religious devotions. Before the city was divided, this day was spent on Mount Sion, up the hill from the Jaffa Gate. There, amid the many memorials, churches, tombs, house of Caiaphas, Armenian Patriarchate, is the Mother of all Catholic churches, the Cenacle. The Upper Room, or Cenacle, is the place where Christ celebrated the Last Supper, instituted the Holy Eucharist, elevated the Apostles to the priesthood and where, at a later date, they received the Holy Spirit on Pentecost. Centuries ago a report was circulated that the body of David was interred beneath the present structure, which has made it treasured by Moslems and Jews. The Cenacle has been in turn Christian church, mosque and a synagogue.

The actual building, constructed as a Gothic church in the twelfth century, became a mosque four centuries ago and a synagogue in

The altar of the Franciscan Chapel of The Cenacle

1949. There are upper and lower churches with the Upper Room being divided into two chambers lighted by fine old windows. This is where Christ supped with his disciples and changed bread and wine into his Body and Blood, celebrating the first Mass. To one side of this room a flight of stairs leads into a cubicle where the Holy Ghost descended on Pentecost day. The lower room, where David is said to have been buried, is the place where Christ washed the Apostles' feet.

The dwelling nearest to the Cenacle was purchased by the Franciscans in the late twenties, who knew the faithful would like to come as close as possible to the sanctuary of the Upper Room. In order that this sacred spot could be seen at all times, the windows back of the little altar were left with clear glass and looked over the courtyard to the old walls. The white stone façade and terrace of this "Franciscan" Cenacle have not altered the original house. Within, tapestry-tiles, pointed arches and a divan—now the chapel—are distinctively Arabic. World-renowned churchmen have come to offer Holy Mass within these walls.

The institution of the Eucharist was preceded by the washing of the feet. This ceremony, observed by each rite, is repeated in the Crusaders' courtyard of the Holy Sepulchre Thursday in Holy Week by the Greek Orthodox. Their Patriarch is celebrant and moves down the lines of distinguished clergymen, Orthodox and Anglican as well as some laymen. He repeats the rite used by Christ, washing and kissing the feet of each one selected. It is a day when the religious communities are especially generous to the mendicants of the city. After the ritual, which draws many because of the rich vestments and the appearance of so many outstanding persons, a visit is made to the Holy Sepulchre, strangely quiet after the hubbub of the throng outside.

When the Passover was finished, Christ left the Upper Room on Mount Sion and crossed the dry brook Cedron to enter a garden,

Ceremony of the Washing of the Feet
in front of the Basilica of the Holy Sepulchre on Maundy Thursday

Clergy at colorful ritual on Holy Thursday

Chanting of the prayers on Holy Thursday

156 *Singing of the passage: "You are not all clean,"
at the Washing of the Feet ritual.
Background upper right, the Mosque of Omar*

Gethsemane. He came to this retreat often and it was known to all the disciples, Judas included. The Paschal moon silvered the earth as Christ, turning to his companions, Peter, James and John, said, "My soul . . . is ready to die with sorrow; do you abide here, and keep watch. So he went forward a little, and fell on the ground, and prayed that if it were possible, the hour might pass him by." Mk. xiv, 34–35. His sufferings increased, sweat fell from his pores in drops of blood. Today this hallowed spot is indicated by a well-kept Grotto, an irregular oval, which has been considered as the place of Judas' betrayal. In the other part of the garden, upon the foundations of the first basilica erected in memory of our Lord's Agony, is the latest church. Dedicated in 1921, the Church of All Nations presents something quite different in the way of building. The roof is formed of twelve small domes—named to honor the Christian nations whose generous offerings made possible the shrine. The building was undertaken by American Catholics who subscribed almost the entire cost of construction. Light diffuses over the spacious interior from unusually elegant purple windows and the altar is highlighted by a newly installed mosaic of the Saviour in Agony. Down before the altar, part of the rock of the Bloody Sweat is seen encircled with a silver crown of thorns, a gift of Australia. Other furnishings include the noble bronze doors, the iron balustrades, gates and the marble carpeting to make this one of the outstanding shrines in Jerusalem. It is used only by the Latin Catholics. The great façade fronting the wide thoroughfare that leads from the Dead Sea Valley to the Holy City is entirely in mosaic, and represents Christ offering his sufferings to his Father.

The garden surrounding one side of the basilica and the monastery holds a special interest because of the eight gnarled olive trees said to have been growing when Christ came here. This may be but a pious legend but there is something impressively ancient about the trees, which still bear fruit and whose leaves are cherished as souvenirs. The remainder of this little plot has been turned into formal paths, bright with flowers known and loved the world over. In reply to a criticism of the garden Chesterton wrote, "The Franciscans have not dared to be reverent; they have only dared to be cheerful."

Gethsemane saw our Blessed Saviour taken prisoner and dragged about Jerusalem in a crude mockery of justice. After He had been seized the Jews took "Jesus into the presence of the high priest, and all the chief priests and elders and scribes were assembled about him." Mk. xiv, 53. That meeting place of the Sanhedrin is now a convent of Armenian Sisters, built on twelfth-century ruins of the ancient markers. It was here the trial of the Saviour began with the questioning by Annas and Caiaphas, high priest of that year. Other nearby sites in the Armenian Quarter show the palace of Caiaphas and a chapel called the Prison of the Lord. The Grotto of St. Peter "in Gallicantu," where he wept bitterly after denying the Lord is not far away.

The climax of the Passion of Jesus is now enshrined within the basilica of the Holy Sepulchre, rallying point of the Crusades, magnet for every lover of the Man of Sorrows. Coming down some steep, slippery stairs, we arrive at the paved court that stretches before the basilica in which place many a Christian was beheaded, and some burnt alive. From the far end of the courtyard rises the façade still showing some of the intricate carving of the Knights. Two massive bays once opened into the interior but Saladin had one blocked up and also two of the upper windows. The precarious condition of the building has necessitated the disfiguring iron scaffolding. Near the open door is the grave of an English nobleman, Sir Philip d'Aubigny (d'Aubeny), sometime tutor to Henry III of England and one of the barons who signed the Magna Carta. The marble slab covering the tomb is finished with a Norman shield and his armorial bearings. That this resting place was not desecrated is due to its being hidden for many years under a stone bench. The small

An arch near the Church of the Holy Sepulchre

159

160 A section of the Church of the Holy Sepulchre, showing the
Crusader's Chapel of the Franks (under small dome).
The original church was dedicated in 335 A.D.

stairway in the right angle of the court leads up to a monumental porch that once opened on to Calvary. When Jerusalem fell in 1187, this was enclosed and a grilled window replaced the door. This is The Chapel of the Franks, dedicated to the Seven Sorrows of Mary.

Entering the gloomy interior of the Holy Sepulchre is an experience not to be forgotten. Just within, on a large divan, are a group of Moslem men busied with several avocations; some making coffee on a spirit stove, another contentedly puffing his *narghile* (water pipe), while another devotee of the Prophet is crouched over the Koran, oblivious to all around. These are the caretakers of the Shrine in whose custody the key to the great doors remains. The religious serving in the sepulchre are locked in after nightfall. When the Turks maintained rulership the burden of taxes for Christians was excessive. Not only were there levies made for each fruit tree but even taxes were demanded when someone died in the Holy Sepulchre. A curious bit of lore tells how the masters were outwitted. An old Friar died in the Holy Sepulchre but the others, not having the means to meet the law, dressed the poor man up, pulled his hood far over his face and with two very much alive confreres taking his arms, as though he were unable to walk, passed between the guardians at the door, tax exempt, on to a respectable burial.

Just to the side of the keepers' divan is the Stone of Unction, placed to mark where Christ's body was prepared for burial. From the great triple candlesticks numerous lamps are hung, the property of three rites, Latin, Greek and Armenian. To the right of the Stone of Unction a door leads into a chapel which is directly under the peristyle of Calvary. Two benches are inside the opening, on the left was the cenotaph of Godfrey, the first King of Jerusalem, and opposite is the tomb of his brother, Baldwin.

By taking the route to the left, the rotunda of the basilica is reached and under the big dome, now trussed with a tangle of supports, is the rectangular Edicule which covers the Tomb of Christ. The exterior is composed of pillars, a balustrade, paintings and lamps which are strung from the corners. The Russian style turret crowning the tomb is hollow and is used for ventilation. The door to the sepulchre is low and narrow and leads into the first of two small chambers. This outer one, the Chapel of the Angel, is called so because it was there that the angel, sitting on the recently rolled away stone, announced the Resurrection. The pedestal in the center of this room contains a fragment of that stone. An even smaller door opens into the adjoining chapel, the Tomb of Christ. All that can be seen in this cell, where three is a crowd, is the slab of marble covering the rock upon which the body of Christ was laid. A profusion of lamps hang from the roof; icons, pictures, and artificial flowers— tokens of the claimants to this shrine—cram the stone ledge just above the cracked marble covering. The odor of incense lingers in the place that has brought such consolation to millions since the day when St. Helena removed the debris and built the first church over the sepulchre of Jesus Christ. That building was long the center of devotion in the city and remained standing until the Persians sacked the Holy Places in 614. The basilica was burnt but not beyond restoration undertaken before 670 by one Modestus, an abbot. He put a roof on the building, built an atrium, a door with two bays and a choir for the high altar. From the eighth to the ninth centuries many chapels were added, both on eastern and western sides. Fire again caused some damage in 966 when defeated Moslems committed this vandalism. In 1010 the Caliph Hakim issued an order that all Christian churches in Palestine, especially the Holy Sepulchre, be destroyed. This edict was but partially obeyed and the lower floor remained unharmed. Two decades later, the defeated Emperor Romanos was ordered to rebuild the destruction. Great sums of money poured in from the Western world as the Emperor Monomachus joined in the labors. When the Crusaders arrived, they

Belfry of the Church of the Holy Sepulchre

Evening procession of Franciscans in the Holy Sepulchre

decided to enrich the holy spot and made substantial changes in the floor plans. Nothing was done after the Moslems retook Jerusalem in the thirteenth century until the fire in 1808, this time accidental. The Greeks, with powers granted by the Sultan, undertook the repairs but the changes introduced were at variance with the former basilican lines. Massive masonry, replaced columns, and walled-up arches turned the church into gloomy chapels, obscuring the view to the Holy Sepulchre. The tomb chapel of native red Palestinian marble was introduced at this time by the Greek architect Comnenos, whose name is on a tablet in the Chapel of the Angel.

The large room across the passage from the entrance to the Tomb itself was once the chapel of the Canons of the Holy Sepulchre, a group of priests dedicated to daily service in this sacred place. Today that space is completely walled in and the wealth of icons can be seen only when the Greek Orthodox are conducting their services. The object in the center of this chapel, a little white ball resting in a shallow dish, is known as the "Center of the World."

In the Church of the Holy Sepulchre almost every form of Christianity gathers to worship God in many tongues—namely, Arabic, Armenian Coptic, Greek, Latin and Syriac. During the liturgies, clergymen of every color and garb are seen officiating in most of the known rites of the Christian churches. Those who claim partial ownership of the basilica are the Greek Orthodox, who have the lion's share of the actual structure; the Latins and the Armenians; while lesser claims are made by Syrians and Copts. On the roof just over St. Helena's chapel are the dwellings of a small number of Abyssinian monks. Other groups such as the Georgians, Maronites and Nestorians once held services within the church but these privileges were forfeited when they could not meet the taxation levied by the Turkish Government in the seventeenth century. There are many small chapels under the roof and these remain in the exclusive use of the sects mentioned. The rotunda, however, is used by all who conduct their functions in the Holy Sepulchre. This entails many administrative difficulties and past history has had many melancholy stories of bickerings and misunderstandings when factions rose. At present, and ever since the British Mandate, the distribution of time allotted for services is arranged and agreed upon by committees representing each rite. They meet with the representative of the government, explain their needs and a list is drawn up from which there can be neither deviation, nor any excuse for the sects running beyond their schedule.

There are clashes on this subject almost always in the years when all the rites celebrate Holy Week simultaneously.

Processions are part of the manifold ceremonies in this basilica. Good Friday the Latins, with all who have been permitted to enter, traverse a lengthy route stopping in many of the chapels in the basilica. There is the chapel of St. Mary Magdalen, just beyond the pillars supporting the dome; the Prison of Christ, once a Jewish tomb; the chapel of St. Longinus, the legionary who thrust his sword into the side of the Crucified; the Column of the Flagellation, where a pillar of broken porphyry is said to be the one on which Christ was bound and scourged; and finally the chapel of St. Helena.

The Chapel of the Finding of the Cross is an underground crypt, many feet below the floor level of the basilica of the Holy Sepulchre, and a little to the right of a chapel named for St. Helena. In this former cistern, tradition says, the Mother of Constantine found three crosses buried under mountainous rubble. The crosses were applied to a sick man and he was cured instantly when touched with the Cross of Christ. The altar in this site is dedicated to the intrepid Queen whose statue, in bronze, is above the altar. The altar table was presented by the Austrian Archduke, Maximilian, who became the ill-fated Emperor of Mexico.

The most sacred places in the Holy Sepulchre come at the end of the journey. Golgotha, the skull-shaped hillock upon which Jesus

Franciscan Superior praying at Stone of Unction,
place of anointing of the Body of Christ

was crucified, is reached by a steep stairway leading to a platform whose adjoining chapels are the property of Greeks and Latins. On the latter side are the places where Christ was stripped of his garments, where He was nailed to the cross, and where his Mother received his lifeless body. The Greek side is more ornate and contains the place of Calvary. Before a silver arch the three figures of the Saviour and the thieves stand out, life-size and realistic. The walls are hidden with icons of rich metals, the roof is decorated with moons, suns and stars. The altar stands over the actual spot of the Crucifixion and that place is shown by a silver disc; the two lateral black marks on either side indicate the crosses of Christ's companions. In this chapel there are always some worshipers in various forms of prayer. Some are heard to groan and sigh, others weep

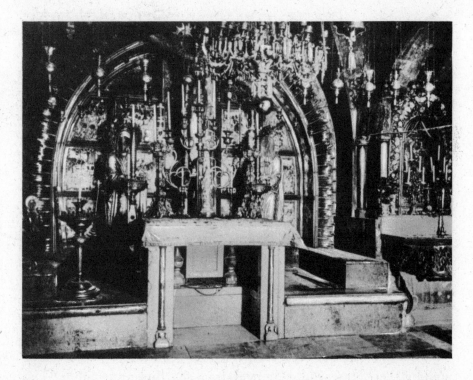

The altar marks the place of the Crucifixion on Mt. Calvary

The Most Rev. Custos of the Holy Land pontificating on the Feast of the Holy Cross in the chapel of the Finding of the True Cross

169

The entrance to Christ's Tomb in the Church of the Holy Sepulchre

silent tears, others with just a casual nod of the head bend to kiss the extended icon and are sprinkled with rose water by one of the Greek monks.

On Good Friday the unusually dramatic Funeral of Christ takes place in the Latin chapel on Calvary. It winds through the rotunda, stopping seven times when a like number of discourses are delivered in as many languages—an attestation of the universality of Redemption. The almost lifelike Crucifix, the finely wrought silver urns, the exquisite needlecraft on linen and vestments are gifts to the Holy Sepulchre from Christian kings and nations. The procession ends in front of the Holy Sepulchre—a vivid reminder of St. Paul's impassioned cry, "God forbid that I should make a display of anything, except the cross of our Lord Jesus Christ." Gal. vi, 14.

Around the rotunda of the basilica there are a series of galleries used by those rites whose lamps festoon the Anointing Stone. This provides an ideal place from which to see the "Fire from Heaven"

170

services conducted by Greek and Armenian rites on Holy Saturday. On either side of the chapel over the Holy Sepulchre are two openings, blackened with the smoke of many years. It is through these holes flaming torches are extended by the Patriarchs of both rites. The faithful of these sects believe that fire is brought from heaven on the eve of Easter and that it is delivered to each prelate praying within the closed tomb. Such a "miracle" does not happen until hours of prayer have caused the thousands crowded into the unlighted church to develop an intense excitement. When the lighted torch does appear there ensues a struggle to be the first to light their tapers and be assured, thereby, of eternal salvation. In what seems to be just a moment the lights glow and the semi-dark rotunda is soon ablaze with flickering Resurrection Fire. The exuberance of the crowd is boundless, another procession forms and in the dense atmosphere, made heavy with the heat of candles and incense, the chanting of the litanies is heard in tones that seem remote, ancient, even weird.

Good Friday morning, and every Friday afternoon, Christians can be seen marching through the cobbled streets of the Old City, part of which is called the Via Dolorosa. The original roadway lies just below the present street. Hence this pilgrim walk, called the Way of the Cross, is merely commemorative. It does honor to fourteen incidents that took place as Christ traveled from the place of condemnation, Pilate's palace, until he arrived on Calvary. Nine of the places marked on this sorrowful journey are supported by Scripture, the others have only the authority of tradition or the outcropping of devotion.

The First Station of the Cross is in what was the Fortress Antonia, where Pontius Pilate, Procurator of Judea, dispensed justice and heard complaints. A police barracks is now in the building over the ruins which show this to have been the Praetorium, and where Pilate condemned Jesus to death. The Second Station is in the Franciscan

The site of the Second Station of the Cross
on the Via Dolorosa

Near the fifth Station of the Cross,
where Simon the Cyrenean helped Jesus carry His Cross

Pilgrims praying at the First Station of the Cross in the Court of Pontius Pilate

Pilgrims carrying a Cross along the Via Dolorosa on Good Friday

174

Chapel of the Condemnation and taking up of the cross. This is erected over the Lithostrotos, where Pilate led the Saviour and presented Him with the introduction, "Behold the Man!" The Third Station is on the Via Dolorosa, where a marble column lying on the ground is the site where Christ fell the first time. Two other such falls are commemorated in the Seventh Station near the Gate of Judgment, upon which His sentence of death was posted, and the Ninth Station in what the Crusaders called "the Street of Bad Cooking" and where there is now a Coptic Church enshrining in the door post a part of a column of early date. The meeting of Mary and Jesus on Good Friday morning is remembered in the Fourth Station, which is an Armenian church, while the Fifth Station, honoring

Christians making the Stations of the Cross
in the streets of the Old City of Jerusalem

Simon of Cyrene, the first known cross-bearer, is in the Street of the Dolors and is marked with a little oratory. The traditional site of the house of Veronica, she who presented a cloth to Christ that He might wipe away the sweat and blood, is the Sixth Station. The fragment of a column in the wall is all that remains, while below the street level an ancient vault has been made into a chapel. On St. Francis Street a Greek Orthodox Church is the Eighth Station, where a group of women seeing the Saviour so bedraggled wept from pity, though this was forbidden by law. Those who were to die could not have any sympathy manifested. The Tenth Station, Christ being stripped of His garments; the Eleventh Station, the nailing to the Cross; the Twelfth Station, death on the Cross; Thirteenth, taking down from the gibbet and the Fourteenth Station, the entombment, are all under the roof of the Holy Sepulchre. As the pious groups

Scene in the Garden of St. Saviour's Convent

St. Saviour's Tower

177

make the Stations the moving verses of the "Stabat Mater," the Passion hymn of Jacopone of Todi, swells on the air and adds the character of sorrow on this Memorial Day.

The domestic instincts of man are strongly appealed to in the Christmas celebrations of the Western world, but it is Easter that causes the Eastern Christians to express their deepest emotions and to proclaim in the Mother-Church of Christendom that Christ is truly risen. Much as one may desire to spend the last days of the year in Bethlehem the impulse to be in the City of Salvation on the days of the tragedy and glory is common to most of the world. No one can realize the depth of emotion that comes into the Christian Orthodox and Uniate in the spring festival when the land is green and the hills have lost their burnt tinge and the olive puts on a freshness.

Easter has a fullness of meaning for the three great faiths—but for such different reasons. For the Jews this is the remembrance of their passing through the Red Sea and into the Promised Land; for the Christians, the culmination of all the miracles of Christ; and, for the Moslems, this is the Nebi Musa (Prophet Moses) celebration. Nebi Musa is that feast which admittedly originated as a Moslem counter-demonstration to the Christian Easter. Fearing that the presence of so many pilgrims in the city might result in some uprising or a Christian coup d'état, Islamic leaders began to have celebrations for one week, preceding the Greek Orthodox Easter, in Jericho, where a tomb is shown and said to be that of Moses. Thousands of eager, zealous Mohammedans still make this pilgrimage and come from all parts of the country, returning to the Holy City just in time for the Orthodox Resurrection and Holy Fire services.

Easter Sunday morning brings the Latin Patriarch into the Holy Sepulchre for the ritual marked with dignity and splendor. The great silver altar is erected just in front of the Tomb of Christ and the con-

178

Marble statue of St. Francis in the courtyard of St. Saviour's Convent

gregation is enlarged by the pilgrims who time their stay to include this Sunday in Jerusalem. The Gospel record is chanted in clear, strong tones, mingling with the rising incense highlighted by the shafts of sun pouring through the windows of the dome. Alleluias resound through the arches as they did in brighter, happier and more liberal days and the spectators are urged by the liturgy "to rejoice and be glad for the Lord has risen as he said, Alleluia." The services finished, the rest of the day is given over to peaceful strolling with friends and visits to some of the other churches in the city.

When all the sites, religious and historical, have been seen and when the mind seems overweighed with details that are confusing though glibly retold by dragoman and guide, when a surfeit with antiquities and ruins benumbs the faculties, then one looks for the relaxing, yet withal pleasing engagements.

Nothing could be more diverting than the people who crowd through the bazaars or market streets of the Old City. Standing in any of these lanes, that are more like long vaulted corridors, and where the merchants sit only two yards apart, one will see more history passing in the various costumes and faces than could be acquired from conning guide books or penciling down the fantastic tales of those who explain the sites. It is an amalgam of conquest and commerce, not unlike the Pentecostal assemblage so well defined by St. Luke (Acts ii, 11) : "There are Partians among us and Medes, and Elamites, our homes are in Mesopotamia, or Judea, or Cappadocia, in Pontus or Asia. Phrygia or Pamphilia, Egypt or the parts of Libya around Cyrene, visitors from Rome . . . Jews . . . and Cretans . . . among us too, and Arabians." God is wonderful in his ways—and in his people.

Coming down the stairway leading into Christian Street is a black-cloaked, bearded man whose uncut hair is twisted into a sort of chignon and above this is a shiny, inverted saucepan of a hat. He is a Greek priest. If he is of a higher rank there will be a gleaming, jewel-

A street scene in the linen market

encrusted medallion and cross suspended from woven chains of gold. The fellahin—those wiry, hardened peasants—shuffle along in their loose footgear, their heads covered with the fringed *kaffiyeh* (large kerchief) and held in place by the *agal*, a binder made of woven goat's hair. The expositors of Islamic law, the mullahs, and the shieks who are chiefs of families or tribes, indicate their rank in the manner of the turbans worn; and their richly woven outer cloaks (*abas*) and decorated vests (*mintians*). The contrast between old

Cobblers in the Old City of Jerusalem

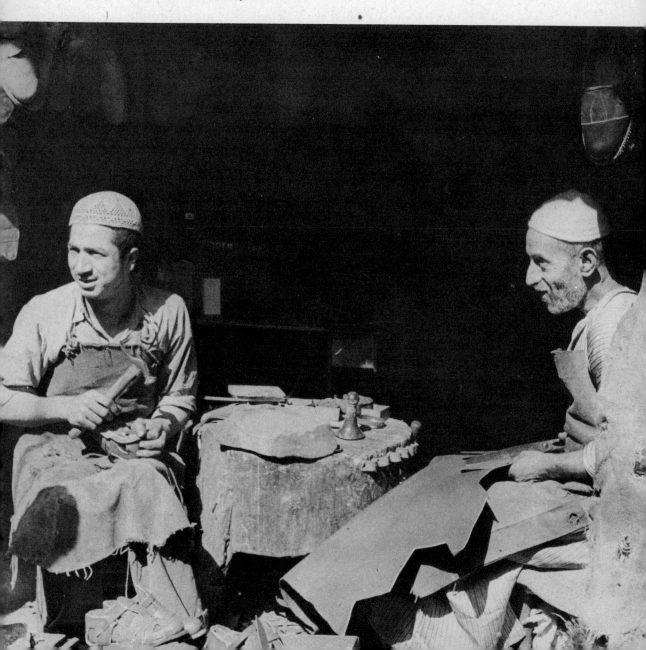

A cobbler

Along Jaffa Road in Israeli Jerusalem

and modern Arabs is seen in their dress. The younger man educated in Western ways will, in all likelihood, remain undistinguished from any other well-dressed gentleman, but his felt tarboosh (fez) will indicate his nationality. There is an alertness in the eyes of these men accustomed to see far distances and their facial characteristics bear traces of tribes who lived in deserts and conquered the shifting sands or who came as Crusaders and remained to rear families. Some of the Arabs are partially bearded, others affect the professional-looking goatee, or the hair-line mustache of the movies. The dark visages, peering from beneath the flowing robes, or the intermediate shades of skin, present unlimited variety. The black-, white-, and brown-robed Latin religious men and the spreading coronets of the Daughters of Charity or the deep blue of the native sisters add the touch of liveliness to the street scenes in the Old City.

In the newer section of Jerusalem, today the territory of Israel, the various outer dress of the Jews is indicative of the historical groups and their features preserve the unblended or mixed strains of racial beginnings. There are Sephardic Jews, whose ancestors were Spanish; the Polish Jews, whose wide-brimmed, fur-edged hats have been immortalized in the richness of Rembrandt's studies; the Ashkenazim of central Europe, still keeping the straggling locks of hair hanging down over the ears; and there are the healthy-looking, shaven Jews of German extraction with an enthusiasm that is contagious. The Balkan types are stodgy, heavy-set people well accustomed to laborious duties and the Yemenites with high cheek bones peer from their shops where intricate silver filigree work is hammered out with a patience that is enviable. Then, there are the American Jews—the tourists who come to visit the Promised Land to discover first hand the vast improvements in a country just beginning its expansion and industrial progress.

The native women strolling along the inclined streets are to be envied by most Western women for their carriage, poise and seren-

Sion Square in New Jerusalem

186

ity. The Bedouin women carry their young children astride one shoulder while balancing a tray on the head or clutching some recent purchase, such as a live chicken. In their long, ruffled, dragging, black formless dresses, their lips tattooed a bluish green, and tribal marks seen on fingers and the backs of the hands, they first cause a feeling akin to pity, but they are happy in their simple way, happy in a home life that is different and they are apparently undisturbed by the latest styles of the tourists. The city Moslem women go completely veiled in public, the village women are not that meticulous. The latter sometimes wear large pieces of cloth about the neck on which are sewn many silver and gold coins—part of their dowry. The display is to indicate how unselfish their husbands are and to create the notion of opulence with such flaunted treasure.

Into this galaxy there is always a sprinkling of officers resplendent with the fancy adjuncts to their impeccably tailored uniforms on which hang all manner of sparkling medals. Children easily slip in and out of the crowds. They doff their tight little white caps, the *takiyeh*, scratch their cropped pates energetically and cry in their practiced, moving way for a baksheesh "in the name of Allah."

This is the Holy City and, while those who dwell therein may not claim sanctity as their personal endowment, they do make the scene kaleidoscopic—and the picture remains long after dates and data have been tucked away as useful but none too important for daily living.

Before leaving the Holy Land we must make two short pilgrimages to previously visited sites where the shrines were then passed over. The first is on Mount Sion. Apart from the Upper Room there is that sacred spot cherished by all who have had devotion for the Mother of Jesus. Among the traditions is one that the Virgin Mary spent her remaining days on this plateau and in the place where she died the Crusaders rebuilt her church, "The Dormition, or The Falling Asleep of the Virgin Mary." Toward the end of the nineteenth

century Kaiser William II bought this land and gave it to the Monks of St. Benedict. The latter began their monumental task of erecting a Romanesque basilica, all the labor, art and design being executed by the religious. The massive walls blend agreeably in the landscape, and the belfry is a beautiful crown to Mount Sion. In the crypt, the place of our Lady's death, there is a recumbent, heroic figure of Mary after the fashion of medieval tombs. The head, hands and feet of the figure are carved from old ivory, which matches the elegance of the gold-overlay design.

Although Mary finished her earthly passage in this spot, her Assumption, that is the union of her body and soul after death, is considered to have taken place in the Valley of Josaphat where the Tomb of the Virgin is located.

This chapel is entered by a steep staircase which ends six feet below in a murky, ill-lighted crypt. Queen Melisande, who is buried in the depths, planned and had this memorial constructed. There is one unique feature of the tomb; there has never been a church built above the Grotto, and it has kept its fifth-century design. The front of the tomb is almost hidden with an Armenian altar and the opening to the right gives access to the sepulchre. There is place for just four persons in the inner chapel, where the tomb is only a little ledge covered by marble. The body of the Virgin Mary was placed here before the Assumption. This has always been the unbroken tradition in all the Oriental churches. The interior of this sepulchre is concealed by stiff, brocaded tapestry falling to pieces. The tomb is guarded daily by one of the Armenian monks, who kindly provide tapers to inspect the underground recess.

Crowning the Mount of Olives is a heavy, square tower, part of the Kaiserin Augusta Victoria Hospice. When Kaiser Wilhelm II of Germany and his wife came to Palestine in 1896 for the dedication of the Lutheran Church of the Redeemer, a reconstructed Crusader church given to his grandfather by the Turkish Sultan, this property

Massive Tower of the Church of the Dormition or "Falling Asleep of the Virgin" on Mt. Sion

was bought and the funds for the building contributed by Germans and their friends. The title to the hospice was given the royal couple on their silver wedding anniversary. In 1910 it was dedicated by Prince Eitel and became a sanitarium; later it was taken by the Mandatory Power government offices. The earthquake of 1927 so damaged the building that it was given up by the English Government and is now a hospital. In the open court the Kaiser and his spouse are represented, in bronze, as Crusaders while in the chapel they are depicted in Byzantine mosaics on the ceiling.

The two lesser Catholic Shrines on the Mount of Olives are the Church of the Pater Noster and Dominus Flevit, where Christ taught the Apostles the "Our Father" and where He looked across the valley and was filled with such sadness that He wept. The former is now a convent of cloistered Carmelite Nuns, who have occupied the place since 1876, when it was purchased, built and given them by a French princess. Visitors enter a cloister with four galleries, around the walls of which are thirty-five frames with the Our Father in different languages. A small building contains the mausoleum of the donor. At the extreme end of the cloister there is an ancient cistern transformed into an oratory called the Crypt of the Credo, but this has been proved to be a legend that grew up in the fourteenth century.

The descent on the rocky road to Gethsemane is marked with a tradition that on this site Jesus "caught sight of the city, and, he wept over it, and said: Ah if thou too couldst understand, above all in this day that is granted thee, the ways that can bring thee peace!" The chapel stands on the site of former churches. In the garden the heart of John Crichton Stuart, Marquis of Bute, has been buried.

This is an ideal place to look across the valley toward the Golden Gate. The large square portal is just before the Temple area and dates from the times of the Empress Eudoxia. Early in the seventh century Heraclius, the Emperor, made his victorious entry and dur-

190

A nun works on altar vestments

The orphans of Jerusalem making vestments and lace
for use in the churches of the Holy Land

ing the Crusader occupancy the Gate was opened twice a year, on Palm Sunday for the Procession and on the fourteenth of September, when a commemoration was made in the liturgy of the Finding of the Holy Cross. The double bays of the Golden Gate are walled up. This was done by Saladin, 1530, to prevent Christians from entering and profaning the Temple area. The dark spots high on the parapet, and which appear in photographs as unidentified blotches, are nothing but weeds that have taken root in the cracked masonry.

There are many fables associated with the Golden Gate. The name has been confused with the "Gate called Beautiful" where Peter and John cured a lame man after Pentecost and it was believed that through these portals Christ rode on Palm Sunday. Another legend says that the next Christian conqueror of Jerusalem shall

A lace worker

ride in triumph by this route. On the outside of the Gate is a badly kept Moslem cemetery used as a grazing place for goats and sheep.

Down in the folds of the Cedron Valley there are four tombs, said to be the resting places of Absalom, David's rebellious son, Josaphat, St. James and St. Zacharias. Seen from above the surrounding graves and markers, this quarter is extremely lugubrious. The tombs have been cut from the reddish granite but are empty of bodies and only the underground darkness can be seen from the outer ledges.

Absalom's Tomb is square and ornamented with Ionic columns holding up a frieze. The upper part is built of blocks and terminates in a circular pyramid. The heap of small stones that are about this tomb are cast by Jews who do this as they pass by because of Absalom's disobedience. In 333, the Pilgrim of Bordeaux writing of two tombs he saw in the Valley called this one the Tomb of Ezechias and another as that of the Prophet Isaias.

The Tomb of Josaphat is a Jewish tomb crowned by a richly ornamented pediment. For almost half a century the entrance has been blocked up by Jews who use this hallowed ground for their deceased.

The Tomb of St. James is another imposing Jewish sepulchre, called by Arabs the Divan of Pharaoh. The columns support Doric bands above the door. There is a suite of burial chambers and a terrace to this tomb. Tradition states that here, after the Crucifixion, St. James went into hiding and was visited by Christ after the Resurrection.

A cubical monolith a few steps away is known to Jews and Christians as the Tomb of Zacharias, to the Arabs as the Tomb of Pharaoh's Wife. Columns adorn the front and the section above the door is terminated with an Egyptian cornice. A pyramid shaped like a quadrangle crowns the tomb.

Olive grove near the Garden of Gethsemane with Tomb of Absalom (center large cone-shaped tomb)

TOWERING over the populous port Haifa is Carmel, on the purple range of mountains with the same name. On its tip is the Stella Maris lighthouse and the guest house maintained by the Carmelite Order. The sides of the mountain are given over to the Jewish residential section, Hadar-Carmel and at its base is the tomb of the founder of Bahaism, Husayn Ali, who was called Baha'ullah, the Splendor of God. Carmel was the abode of Elias the prophet and thither came the soldiers of Napoleon, many of whom are buried in a common grave near the bastion-like monastery. Over the great altar is the richly carved statue Lady of Mt. Carmel, while below is the cave-dwelling of the Prophet who defeated the priests of Baal and incurred the wrath of Jezabel (III Kings, xviii). Visitors find the mountain to be as pictured by Isaias, it—"thrills the barren desert with rejoicing; the wilderness takes heart and blossoms fair as the lily . . . all the majesty of Lebanon is bestowed on it." Isai. xxxv, 1–2.

CONCLUSION

IT HAS BEEN OFTEN SAID in Palestine that one who comes for a fortnight's stay usually returns to his home and authors a most readable, authentic guide book. One who remains for a year just busies himself collecting material for his project, but the one who lives in Palestine for a longer period becomes so enthusiastic about the country that all thoughts of writing give place to an appreciation and gratitude for being in the land of the Saviour, and the enthusiasm makes one inarticulate.

Thus the writer of this little commentary does not find it an easy task to speak of "the Arcady of the East." Anyone who has seen a sunset over the Mountains of Moab; spent the early hours of the day on Tabor; or passed some time on the Carmel range can never forget the urge and the inability to express those Te Deum sentiments "reaching far beyond the confines of this little world."

A visit to the Catholic Shrines of the Holy Land—and there are many others equally interesting—presumes an enthusiasm and a sympathy, a placid understanding in order that the wheat of facts may be sifted from the chaff of fiction. Only then will the consequence of Messianic association be appraised and remembered.

Going up to Mt. Sion in Jerusalem, walking over the Shepherds' Field near Bethlehem, making a prayer in Nazareth, sailing on the Lake of Galilee, shopping in any of the exotic bazaars, watching a shepherd guide his flock through the maze of motor traffic in Haifa or trying to avoid persistent dragomans, around the hotels, one discovers this is the land of contrasts, "built . . . in fellowship. There the tribes meet, the Lord's own tribes, to give praise . . . to the Lord's name." Ps. cxxi, 3–4.

There lingers in the purple shadows of Gethsemane and in the incense-laden air of Calvary, around the quiet shore of Galilee and in the mute ruins of Capharnaum, a peace which surpasses all understanding. And if "we wonder at the way in which they (Palestinians) seem to gild the lily they would wonder much at the way we gild the weed." The episodic highlights of the Saviour's sojourn— three crowded years—are kept alive in shrine and sanctuary, meadow and mountain. He cannot be forgotten. All generations must take a stand concerning him—Christ Jesus. "My kingdom," he stated, "does not belong to this world." (Jo. xviii, 36.) But his life, labor and love hallowed this strip of land which is called, and for such a good reason, *the* Holy Land. With the rising cadences of hymn and psalm there comes a prayerful petition, "Jerusalem, if I forget thee, perish the skill of my right hand! Let my tongue stick fast to the roof of my mouth if I cease to remember thee . . . the fountain-head of my content." Ps. cxxxvi, 5.

BIBLIOGRAPHY

ADDISON, J. T.
 The Christian Approach to the Moslem, Columbia University Press, New York, 1942.

BARTLETT, W. H.
 Jerusalem Revisited, Hall, Virtue & Co., London, 1855.

BELLOC, HILAIRE
 The Crusades, Bruce and Co., Milwaukee, 1937.

BURTON, LADY ISABEL
 The Inner Life of Syria, Palestine, and the Holy Land, H. S. King, London, 1884.

CHESTERTON, G. K.
 The New Jerusalem, Hodder and Stoughton, London, 1920.

CONDOR, C. R.
 The Latin Kingdom of Jerusalem, Palestine Exploration Fund, London, 1897.

DANIEL-ROPS
 Sacred History, Longmans, Green & Co., New York, 1949.

FAWCETT, DAME MILLICENT
 Easter in Palestine, C. F. Unwin, London, 1926.

FILLION, REV. L. C.
 Life of Christ, 3 vols., B. Herder & Co., St. Louis, 1929.

GRAVES, PHILIP
 Palestine, the Land of Three Faiths, Jonathan Cape, London, 1923.

HANAUER, REV. J. E.
 Walks in and Around Jerusalem, Church Mission to the Jews, London, 1926.

HICHENS, ROBERT
 The Holy Land, The Century Co., New York, 1910.

HOLMES, JOHN HAYNES
 Palestine Today and Tomorrow, Macmillan Co., New York, 1929.

HUGHES, PHILIP
 A Popular History of the Catholic Church, Macmillan Co., New York, 1949.

KNOX, MSGR. RONALD
 Old Testament in English, Sheed & Ward, New York, 1948.

KNOX, MSGR. RONALD
 New Testament in English, Sheed & Ward, New York, 1946.

KRAELING, CARL H.
 Gerasa, City of the Decapolis, American Schools of Oriental Research, New Haven, 1938.

LAMB, HAROLD
 The Crusades, Garden City Publishing Co., Garden City, 1930.

LEEN, REV. EDWARD
 In the Likeness of Christ, Sheed & Ward, London, 1936.

LEGENDRE, ADOLPH A. C.
 The Cradle of the Bible, B. Herder, St. Louis, 1929.

LOTI, PIERRE
 Jerusalem, T. Werner Laurie, London.

LUKE, SIR HARRY AND KEITH-ROACH, EDWARD
 The Handbook of Palestine and Trans-Jordan, Macmillan Co., London, 1934.